AIR TRAFFIC CONTROL
TODAY & TOMORROW

AIR TRAFFIC CONTROL TODAY & TOMORROW

Anne Paylor

IAN ALLAN
Publishing

CONTENTS

First published 1993

ISBN 0 7110 2137 6

Published by Ian Allan Ltd, Shepperton, Surrey; and printed by Ian Allan Printing Ltd at their works at Coombelands in Runnymede, England.

Page 2: The dramatic control tower at Paris Charles de Gaulle airport dominates a Douglas DC-9, G-BMAI, of British Midland Airways.
AUSTIN J. BROWN/AVIATION PICTURE LIBRARY

Below: A Douglas DC-9, OY-KIB, of SAS is pictured alongside the terminal building at Düsseldorf, with the airport's control tower in the background.
AUSTIN J. BROWN/AVIATION PICTURE LIBRARY

Opposite: Interior of the Apron Control at Prestwick Airport in October 1992.
AUSTIN J. BROWN/AVIATION PICTURE LIBRARY

ABBREVIATIONS

(A)VASI — (Abbreviated) Visual Approach Slope Indicators
ACC — Area Control Centre
ADF — Automatic Direction Finder
ADS — Automatic Dependent Surveillance
AFTN — Aeronautical Fixed Telecommunications Network
ATC — Air Traffic Control
ATCC — Air Traffic Control Centre
ATIS — Automated Terminal Information Services
ATS — Air Traffic Services
CAA — Civil Aviation Authority
CCF — Central Control Function
CTA — Control Area
(D)VOR — (Doppler) Very High Frequency Omni-Directional Radio Range
DME — Distance Measuring Equipment
FAA — Federal Aviation Administration (US)
FANS — Future Air Navigation Systems
FIR — Flight Information Region
GLONASS — Global Orbiting Navigation Satellite System
GNSS — Global Navigation Satellite System
GPS — Global Positioning System
HF — High Frequency
ICAO — International Civil Aviation Organisation
ILS — Instrument Landing System
INS — Inertial Navigation System
LATCC — London Air Traffic Control Centre
MLS — Microwave Landing System
Mode S — Mode Select
NDB — Non-Directional Beacon
PAPI — Precision Approach Path Indicators
PAR — Precision Approach Radar
RVR — Runway Visual Range
SA — Selective Availability
ScOATCC — Scottish Air Traffic Control Centre
Selcal — Selective Calling
SSR — Secondary Surveillance Radar
STOL — Short Take-off and Landing
TCAS — Traffic Collision Avoidance Systems
TMA — Terminal Control (or Manoeuvring) Area
UHF — Ultra High Frequency
VHF — Very High Frequency

1. INTRODUCTION

Congestion remains the key problem facing Europe's air traffic as the century races to a close. Air traffic control (ATC) delays now account for approximately 80% of all flight delays and it seems unlikely that any significant improvements can be achieved in the short term.

Two industry-generated reports — *A European Planning Strategy for Air Traffic to the Year 2010* published by the International Air Transport Association (IATA) in 1990 and *Towards a Single System for Air Traffic Control in Europe* published by the Association of European Airlines (AEA) in 1989 — highlighted that congestion was costing the airline industry US$5 billion a year in 1989. This was expected to rise to US$10 billion by the year 2000 if nothing was done.

To minimise the effect of delays on their customers, airlines in Europe are estimated to be flying approximately 13% more air miles than they need to, and this entails heavy investment in surplus capacity. According to an IATA study, total delays in June 1992 were equivalent to the grounding of 30 aircraft for a whole month.

The reports also concluded that, unless improvements were implemented urgently, the European air traffic system would be unable to cope with increases in air transport beyond 1995.

But with closer European co-operation following the introduction of the Single Market at the beginning of 1993, there are moves to rationalise Europe's airspace so that it will be able to handle larger numbers of aircraft in greater safety.

The UK airspace is a key part of the overall European system and boasts some of the busiest traffic sectors within the European Community. In London Heathrow, it has the busiest European airport, and it enjoys a very high standard of air traffic services to cope with such density of traffic.

Indeed, the airways between London and Paris are the busiest in Europe, with Frankfurt also recording extremely high traffic levels.

But the inexorable growth in traffic is predicted to continue, with industry analysts anticipating an annual average growth rate of just over 5% to the end of the century. Since 1986, there has been a 40% growth in traffic and, despite the small hiccup caused by recession and compounded by the ripple effects of the Gulf conflict of 1991, growth is now almost back on target and 1986 traffic levels are expected to have doubled by the turn of the century.

Above: **The sun glints off the tail of a BAe 146 as it climbs out after take-off.**

Above right: **A Cathay Pacific 747-300 climbs away.**

Right: **A pilot's eye view of the runway as the aircraft begins its take-off run.**

Indeed, there are expectations that, having taken more than 40 years to notch up its one billionth passenger since the commercial air transport industry can really be said to have established itself after World War 2, the global airline community is expected to take just 10 years to notch up its second billion by the year 2000. Just five years on from that, air travel is anticipated to have become so commonplace that the industry will notch up its third billionth passenger in 2005.

Europe alone is expected to be handling 1.1 billion passengers by the year 2010, compared to just 394 million in 1990.

Such growth and such large numbers of people travelling around the skies are almost beyond imagination. If the infrastructure in place today, which in essence dates back decades, cannot cope with today's traffic levels, how will it cope with the sort of densities forecast for 2005 and beyond? Many of

Europe's top airports are already bursting at the seams, but population densities and environmental constraints mean that most European countries are unable to add the runway capacity necessary or build new airports to cope with the additional passengers and aircraft.

But there is a new global aviation order taking shape, one that could in effect become the first to overcome national boundaries and evolve a truly international industry. The following chapters serve to investigate some of the prime movers of that order and some of most significant elements, particularly as they relate to Europe and therefore to the United Kingdom.

2. AIR TRAFFIC CONTROL

The primary function of air traffic control (ATC) is to prevent collisions between aircraft, both in the air and on the ground at airports. But in order to do this, controllers must know where the aircraft are, so most air traffic is channelled into designated zones and airways. These are known as 'controlled airspace', indicating a positive level of air traffic control in which controllers rather than pilots assume responsibility for collision avoidance (although the pilot ultimately retains responsibility for the safety of his aircraft and any passengers and crew on board). Aircraft operating in controlled airspace may only do so with the permission of the control authorities, and must be suitably equipped — usually with some form of instrument capability, but at the very least with air/ground radio communications links.

Controlled Airspace

Controlled airspace consists of 'Control Zones' established around major airports, which stretch from the surface to a specified altitude; the various 'Airways' which are 10nm-wide corridors in the sky, created to expedite the flow of commercial air transport between major airports; and 'Terminal Control (or Manoeuvring) Areas' (TMAs), which are much larger than Control Zones and are established where airways intersect in the vicinity of Control Zones.

Overlapping the upper level of the Control Zone and the lower level of the TMA is a transition level. As a general rule, for ATC purposes, all 'zones' cover a tract of airspace which starts at the surface and

Above: **A Swissair MD-11 taking off.**
MCDONNELL DOUGLAS

Left: **An Icelandair Boeing 757.**
ICELANDAIR

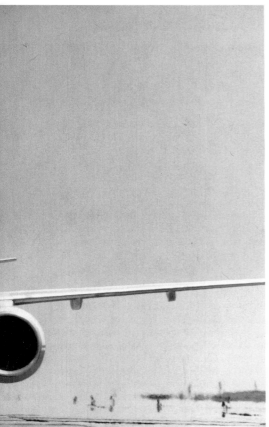

extends to a specified height (usually 3,000ft). Control 'areas' on the other hand start at a specified height above the surface (2,000ft, for example) and extend upwards to a specified ceiling. In the United States, however, some TMAs (or TCAs 'Terminal Control Areas' as they are known there), extend from the surface to a specified upper level.

In addition to controlled airspace, there are other areas designated as 'Advisory Airspace', 'Special Rules Airspace', 'Aerodrome Traffic Zones', and 'Military Aerodrome Traffic Zones' (MATZ) which offer a range of air traffic services and require ATC clearances. There are also various types of restricted airspace, some permanent and some only temporary, which normally relate to military activity, either on the ground or airborne training.

Large tracts of European airspace are dedicated to military activity, especially over Germany which has been occupied by four foreign armies — the UK, the US, France, and Russia — since the end of the last war. Much of the German airspace has been carved up to allow training areas for the fighter aircraft of the various air forces.

With the collapse of the Eastern Bloc, there has been much greater demand for civil access to military airspace and, indeed, there is now much more co-operation between the two. Countries like Denmark

have abolished military airspace altogether with a single civil authority providing all air traffic services to civil and military operations alike. Training areas are allocated when necessary and on a temporary basis: once the training requirement has been met, the airspace reverts to full civil use.

This is a growing trend and, as civil airspace becomes ever more congested, there will inevitably be more civil access to military airspace. But while co-operation increases, it is also true that today's fighter aircraft are such high performance machines that they need ever larger areas in which to train. At the sort of speeds at which they are operating, a single manoeuvre may eat up a large chunk of airspace. In addition, these high performance aircraft have very short operational range capabilities. It is, therefore, not possible for them to travel to a remote training location without refuelling, so training sites have to be as close as possible to their home bases.

Separations

In all controlled airspace, aircraft travel at predetermined vertical and lateral separations.

Separations are the minimum safe distances that should be maintained between aircraft as defined by the International Civil Aviation Organisation (ICAO). ICAO is the regulatory body governing international air transport. There are a number of variables affecting separations.

These include, for example, the presence or absence of radar surveillance, the integrity and reliability of radio communications services, and the level of navigation and communications equipment carried on board the aircraft.

Above: **A Japan Airlines Boeing 747-400 at sunset.**
JAPAN AIRLINES

Below right: **The control tower at Dublin Airport.**

For take-off and landing, separations vary according to the types of aircraft and the visibility levels on the ground. Jets, for example, generate wake turbulence which can be a very real hazard for lighter aircraft. So if a light aircraft is landing or taking off behind a jet, the controller will usually allow at least an extra mile's separation over the gap for one jet following another.

Even in the air, wake turbulence or 'jet wash' can be felt as a fairly severe pocket of turbulence if even a widebodied jet passes close behind another.

In the airways, vertical separation is generally maintained through application of the semicircular rule under which all aircraft on a magnetic track of 000° to 179° fly at odd thousand feet while those on a heading of 180° to 359° fly at even thousand feet, giving a vertical separation between aircraft travelling in the same direction of 2,000ft except above 29,000ft where the interval between levels is increased to 4,000ft.

Below 24,500ft and in uncontrolled airspace, a quadrantal rule applies. Under this rule, aircraft flying on a magnetic track of 000° to 089° should fly at odd thousand feet, between 090° and 179° at odd thousands plus 500ft, between 180° and 269° at even thousand feet, and between 270° and 359° at even thousands plus 500ft.

Uncontrolled Airspace

Uncontrolled airspace is anything outside Control Zones or other restricted airspace and beneath the airways which usually start at 5,000ft and have an upper limit of about 25,000ft. In uncontrolled airspace, aircraft need be equipped with only the bare minimum of navigation equipment and need have no instrument capability at all. Indeed, in many countries including the UK it is not even a requirement that all aircraft are fitted with radio.

As long as a pilot observes the rules of the air and keeps out of controlled or restricted airspace, he need make no contact with air traffic services at all. Where there is radar coverage, air traffic controllers will be aware of all aircraft operating in their airspace whether or not they are communicating with them. As a result, traffic advisory and information services are available in uncontrolled airspace, but the responsibility for collision avoidance rests solely with the pilot.

For the purposes of air traffic control, there are three categories of aircraft operating heights, each of which attracts its own distinct terminology. Aircraft gauge their height through use of an instrument that measures air pressure: the altimeter. However, air pressure is constantly changing throughout the day and in different parts of the country. As a result, pressure settings have been standardised into three categories.

Of the three, 'QFE' is the most localised pressure setting and relates to the actual atmospheric pressure at an airport. When an aircraft is intending to land at a particular airport, the air traffic controller will notify the pilot of the 'QFE' at that airport. By readjusting the pressure setting on his altimeter, the pilot will have an accurate indication of his height for the local pressure levels, and will have a zero reading on his altimeter when he lands. In the US, such pressure settings are not commonly used and the pilot must know the height above sea level of the airfield in order to calculate the correct approach profile. While flying on the 'QFE', the aircraft is operating at a 'height' or vertical distance above the airport.

The 'QNH' is usually used on departure from an airport and provides a pressure reading which is an average taken from all the pressure gauges within a designated region. There are some 20 altimeter setting regions in the UK and each calculates a mean pressure setting for that whole region. 'QNH' settings are usually used up to the Transition Altitude (the height at which aircraft switch on to a standard world-wide pressure setting), which is usually about 5,000ft, but can in reality be anything from 2,000ft to 18,000ft, depending on the local civil aviation regulations. All flights on 'QNH' settings operate at 'altitudes' not heights. Altitude represents the vertical distance of the aircraft above mean sea level.

Above the transition altitude, all aircraft adopt the standard pressure setting of 1013.2 millibars, which means that all flights operating in the airways are using the same pressure settings and are therefore all using the same height reference data. All heights are now referred to as 'flight levels' and for ATC communications purposes only the first three numbers of the figure are used. Flight level (FL) 26,000ft therefore becomes FL260, and FL 9,000ft becomes FL090.

3. AIR TRAFFIC CONTROL IN THE UK

Air traffic services within UK airspace are provided by the National Air Traffic Services (NATS) which is an organisation jointly responsible to the Civil Aviation Authority (CAA) and the Ministry of Defence (MoD). As such, it provides air traffic services (ATS) to both civil and military air traffic, and is also responsible for the planning, provision and maintenance of such essential ATS equipment as radar, navigational aids and communications systems.

For the purposes of air traffic control, UK airspace is divided into two 'Flight Information Regions'

(FIRs) which are controlled from the nation's three air traffic control centres.

The London FIR, which incorporates most of England and Wales up to 55° North as well as the surrounding seas up to the boundary of the Isle of Man, Northern Ireland and the airspace of adjacent countries, is controlled from two 'Air Traffic Control Centres' (ATCCs), the main one of which is the London Air Traffic Control Centre or LATCC which is based at West Drayton, not far from Heathrow Airport.

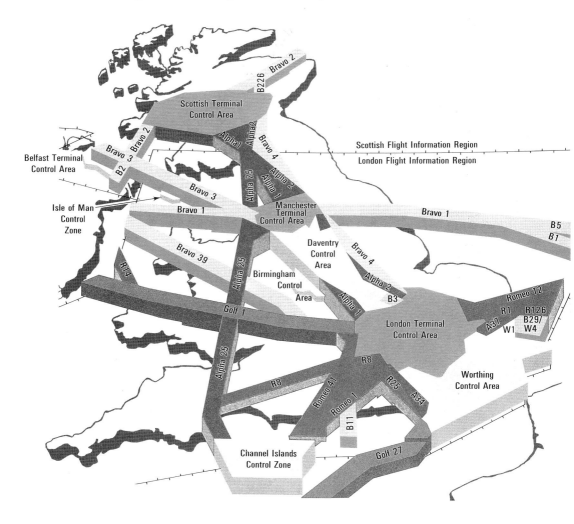

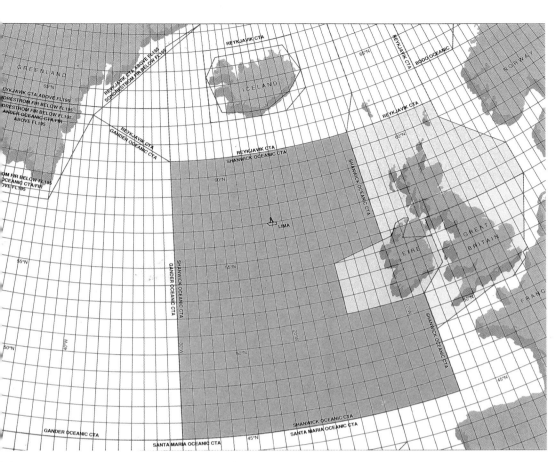

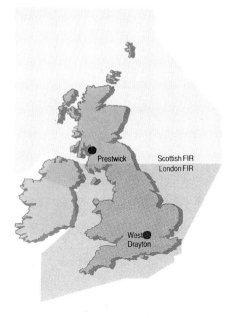

Left: The airways system above the UK. Air traffic control for the whole of the UK is provided by the National Air Traffic Service (NATS).
CAA

Above: Control of the northern Atlantic Ocean is shared by the US (Gander Oceanic CTA), Iceland (Reykjavik CTA), the UK (Shanwick Oceanic CTA), and Portugal (Santa Maria Oceanic CTA). The Shanwick region is a joint operation provided by ScOATCC in Prestwick with communications provided by the Irish control centre in Shannon.
CAA

Right: The UK's upper airspace is divided into two Flight Information Regions (FIRs): the London FIR controlled from the London Air Traffic Control Centre (LATCC) at West Drayton; and the Scottish FIR controlled from the Scottish Air Traffic Control Centre (ScOATCC) in Prestwick.
CAA

13

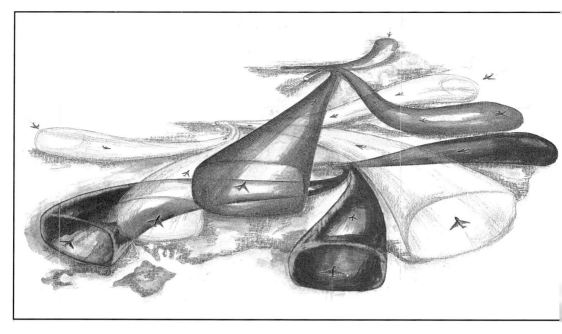

Above: **The CCF 'tunnels in the sky' concept is aimed at increasing airspace in the southeast of England by up to 30%.** CAA

Right: **The UK Civil Aviation Authority's New En Route Centre at Fareham in Hampshire is due to open in 1996.** CAA

Originally established as a sub-centre to LATCC, handling aircraft flying below 15,500ft in the airways system around Manchester and over the Irish Sea, the air traffic control unit serving Manchester International Airport was in 1993 upgraded to full ATCC status, covering an area stretching from Birmingham to Carlisle and from the Isle of Man into the North Sea. Its area of jurisdiction now reaches to 17,500ft and when the new 'Central Control Function' (CCF) comes on line in 1995, Manchester's control ceiling will be lifted to 19,500ft to match CCF's upper limit.

Air traffic control services for the Scottish FIR are provided by the 'Scottish and Oceanic Air Traffic Control Centre' (ScOATCC), located at Prestwick, which is responsible for all traffic in an area which stretches from 55°N to 61°N almost reaching the Faroe Islands and almost 250 miles to the east to the boundaries of the Norwegian and Danish FIRs, and about 150 miles to the west, taking in the airspace over Northern Ireland.

Between them, LATCC and ScOATCC provide air traffic services for all aircraft flying *en route* above 17,500ft (19,500ft after 1995) in UK airspace. Each centre is manned by both civil and military controllers who provide advisory and information services when requested in addition to their standard air traffic control functions. Manchester is purely a civil operation.

In addition to providing domestic ATC services, ScOATCC also provides air traffic control over the eastern sector of the North Atlantic, a responsibility assigned to the UK by the ICAO.

This a densely trafficked region because it is home to the major and most heavily used air routes linking Europe with the US. Because most airlines wish to take advantage of favourable winds and optimise route efficiency by following the 'Great Circle Route', most flights between the European continent and the United States route over the northern sector of the Atlantic, following airways which channel them from Scotland or Ireland to just south of Iceland, skirting the southern tip of Greenland, and entering North American airspace over Newfoundland or Labrador.

Most of this airspace is over vast expanses of water and, because of the physical limitations of radar range (little more than 200nm), there can be no visual monitoring of the whereabouts of aircraft. All oceanic air traffic control is therefore 'procedural' (voice or data communications only) using position reports and estimates passed from the aircraft to the controllers to establish that aircraft's whereabouts. Under procedural control, separations between aircraft must be greater than those required when radar surveillance is possible, to allow a great margin of error. This in turn means that fewer aircraft can operate in that airspace at the same time, reducing its capacity. As traffic levels over the North Atlantic continue to increase, a shortage of airspace capacity during peak periods is becoming a problem.

Responsibility for the vast North Atlantic region is shared by the UK, Portugal, the US, Canada, and Iceland. From ScOATCC, controllers provide procedural air traffic services in an area known as the Shanwick CTA in which communications facilities are provided by the Irish authorities in Shannon. The area stretches west to 30°W, north to 61°N, and south to 41°N where it joins Portugal's Santa Maria Oceanic CTA. In this region, all communications between pilots and controllers are channelled through a high frequency radio station near Shannon in Ireland.

To provide the best possible routeing for aircraft over the North Atlantic, a system of organised tracks is created by the relevant OACC every 12hr. The Prestwick OACC is responsible for drawing up the optimum westbound tracks, while Gander in Canada handles the eastbound track system.

Within each of the FIRs, there are two main categories of airspace: controlled and uncontrolled. In uncontrolled airspace, aircraft may fly when and where they like subject to the UK's air laws, which cover such things as licensing and the privileges thereof, procedures to be observed by all pilots, VFR ('Visual Flight Rules') and IFR ('Instrument Flight Rules')

minima, and the airworthiness of aircraft.

Visual Flight Rules are applied when weather conditions are such that the pilot can safely maintain visual separation from obstacles or other aircraft: known as 'Visual Meteorological Conditions' (VMC). In essence VFR minima relate to visibility and both vertical and horizontal clearance of cloud.

Instrument Flight Rules govern operations during 'Instrument Meteorological Conditions' (IMC) when weather conditions make it impossible for the pilot to maintain visual separation or reference. Any pilot must then rely on flying by instrument. He will require at least some degree of instrument capability in order to fly in controlled airspace.

In controlled airspace — Control Zones, Terminal Control Areas, airways and other special areas — aircraft are subject to the direction of air traffic controllers.

CCF

The southeastern corner of the UK is one of the most densely trafficked sectors of airspace in the world. It is home to the three London airports: Heathrow, which is the UK's major international gateway facility and is

Left: The Central Control Function operations room at the London Air Traffic Control Centre (LATCC), West Drayton.
CAA

Below: Radar displays at LATCC have switched from the traditional horizontal type....
CAA

Right: .... to vertical displays, as pictured here at the Heathrow Approach sector at LATCC.
CAA

Below right: The Heathrow Tower, or Visual Control Room, handles up to 70 movements an hour.
CAA

still the busiest international airport in the world, Gatwick and Stansted, as well as the newer London City Airport in Docklands and Luton Airport in Bedfordshire. In addition, the region is littered with general aviation airfields, busy military airbases (including Northolt and Farnborough), and is handling a growing amount of executive jet traffic using such sites as Biggin Hill.

In terms of the air traffic control workload, the whole of the southeast of England has been described as one giant Terminal Control Zone.

And, despite the success of many other regional airports and Manchester in particular in establishing themselves as real regional alternatives, demand for access to the London system and Heathrow in particular continues to grow.

To handle the increasing traffic, the CAA is investing £750 million in new equipment and systems to increase airspace capacity and facilitate greater integration with Europe.

In the southeast, the most significant change is the introduction of the Central Control Function — CCF. Also known as 'tunnels in the sky', CCF completely changes the way traffic in the London TMA is handled, from geographical sectors to a more centralised system.

At present, traffic in the London TMA is controlled from LATCC and arriving flights, for example, are directed to the designated holding point for whichever London airport that flight is scheduled to land at. From

the holding point, the airport's localised approach controllers assume responsibility for the final part of the flight, guiding the aircraft into the approach sequence, and handing over to tower controllers for the landing sequence.

Since the tower controller is the only one who actually establishes visual contact with that aircraft, there is no particular necessity for the approach controller to be located at the airport. By bringing all

the area and approach controllers together in one operations centre, it is hoped that CCF will streamline liaison between TMA and approach controllers, reduce handovers, improve efficiency, and thereby increase capacity within the southeast system.

Under the old system, the TMA was divided into a series of three-dimensional blocks or sectors with a team of controllers maintaining separations between the flows of traffic within their sectors as they criss-crossed the various inbound and outbound routes.

Under CCF, which is due to be fully operational by the end of 1995, the total TMA airspace will be organised into dedicated and separated departure and arrival routes for each of the airports. The controlled sectors will then take the form of tunnels in the sky and each controller will be responsible for traffic which is crossing his sector in a single direction only. It simplifies the controller's job and improves efficiency — thereby increasing capacity over southeastern England by a significant 30%.

CCF will be based at West Drayton, and the Heathrow and Gatwick approach control functions were moved to the centre in early 1993. Stansted approach will be moved to the CCF Operations Centre as soon as traffic levels at that airport demand.

NERC

Meanwhile, the *en route* functions currently based at LATCC will be relocated to the £200 million New En Route Centre (NERC) currently under construction at Fareham in Hampshire.

Due to be fully operational by 1996, NERC will handle all *en route* flights in UK airspace currently handled by LATCC, except for those within the CCF area, and will interface with ScOATCC. New equipment, streamlined procedures, and a more centralised approach should generate airspace capacity increases of up to 40%.

NERC will feature the largest operations room in

Europe, if not the world, and will require a total workforce of about 900 people, including up to 500 air traffic controllers providing 24hr coverage of the London FIR airspace.

RADREP

The third major element of the CAA's upgrade investment is the Scottish Radar Replacement Programme. This includes re-equipping and refurbishing the radar sites at Lowther Hill and Aberdeen, and the installation of a new radar site to the north of Aberdeen to provide cover for helicopter operations serving the North Sea oil industry.

Radar facilities at Glasgow and Edinburgh airports are also being upgraded.

Manpower

In the mid-1980s, the CAA/NATS recognised that the development of NERC, the move to the CCF, and general traffic growth would generate an increasing demand for additional trained manpower. At that time, recruitment was running at approximately 50 trainees per year, of whom 55-60% qualified from classroom training and went on to work at airports or in the centres.

However, manpower planning indicated that, by 1990/91, up to 180 new controllers would be needed each year for the operational ATC units. Recruiting levels have accordingly been stepped up and are reflected in the number of trainee controllers delivered

to the operational units since 1989. That year, there were just 30, with an increase to 50 for 1990, a significant leap to 135 in 1991, and a massive 192 in 1992, bringing the countrywide total of controllers to 1,324, which is about 60 short of the total requirement at the end of 1992. Some 212 new trainees were due to be recruited in 1993 and, currently, up to 300 trainees are under initial training at any one time.

In a bid to try and speed up the training process, the

Above left: **Heathrow was one of the earliest airports to install ground movement radar. The system has consistently been upgraded and provides an invaluable safety enhancement during bad weather when visibility is impaired.**
CAA

Left: **One of the civil sectors — the Daventry sector — at LATCC.**
CAA

Above: **The sub-centre at Manchester Airport has now been upgraded to full centre status within the London FIR.**
MANCHESTER AIRPORT

Right: **Heathrow remains the busiest international airport in the world, attracting airlines from all regions.**
BAA PLC

UK has switched from dual discipline training (whereby recruits are trained to be able upon completion of their ATC classroom training to work at both an airport and a centre) to single discipline training. Under this system, the recruit trains for either an airport or centre rating, reducing training time from three years to just 18 months. The drawback is that there is less flexibility in the single discipline system and controllers are leaving college less 'ATC mature'

While NATS controllers provide all *en route* and approach services, as well as ATC for many of the

country's top airports, some smaller airports and many general aviation airfields use the services of controllers provided by independent suppliers. These companies recruit and train their own air traffic controllers to full CAA standards and contract out their services.

RUCATSE

In response to a request from the Secretary of State for Transport in 1988 for advice on a number of aspects of air traffic distribution and future airspace and airport capacity, the Civil Aviation Authority in February

Above: **The Heathrow control tower with the visual control room on top.**

Below: **International carriers line up outside Manchester's new Terminal 2.**
MANCHESTER AIRPORT

1989 published a document (CAP 548) entitled *Traffic Distribution Policy for the London Area and Strategic Options for the Long Term*. In that document, the CAA noted that a new runway for the London area was likely to be needed by about the year 2000, and that planning should begin immediately. Without giving consideration to any greenfield site options, the CAA was asked to recommend a range of runway options in what became known as the RUCATSE (Runway Capacity for the South East) study.

The options, as proposed in CAP 570 — *Traffic Distribution Policy and Airport and Airspace Capacity: the Next 15 Years* — which was published in the summer of 1990, include the following:

- a third full or STOL (short take-off and landing) runway at Heathrow;
- a second runway at Gatwick;
- a second runway at Stansted;
- further development of existing runway capacity at Luton Airport;
- or making greater use of the existing airports at Bristol, Southampton, Bournemouth, and Lydd with 'sectorisation' — permitting each airport to handle traffic from one general direction only and thereby keeping the bulk of traffic away from the London TMA.

Other options included the exclusion of small (less than 80 seats) aircraft from Heathrow, Gatwick and Stansted, or the introduction of fixed charges for all air transport movements at the London airports in a bid to encourage airlines to use larger aircraft and thereby reduce the number of movements.

Since the publication of Cap 570, there has been no further progress on the RUCATSE question. But, in view of the long lead times involved in runway construction, if planning does not begin soon, London will be unable to meet air transport demand into the next century and will inevitably lose its status as the world's busiest international air transport hub to rival airports in continental Europe.

4. EUROPEAN AIRSPACE

Defining Europe's airspace is a task on its own and, as its borders are ever mobile, those definitions are constantly changing. At present, there are 12 members of the European Community: Belgium, Denmark, France, Germany, Greece, Ireland, Italy, Luxembourg, the Netherlands, Portugal, Spain, and the UK.

There is some considerable debate as to whether the market should be allowed to expand to include the recently liberated Eastern European republics, and there are other countries, such as Norway and Sweden, which are considering membership and have already adopted many of the Single Market practices.

Of the 12 core EC members, nine (Germany, France, the UK, the Netherlands, Belgium, Luxembourg, Greece, Ireland, and Portugal) are members of the European Organisation for the Safety of Air Navigation, or Eurocontrol — which was established in 1960 with the ultimate aim of providing upper airspace air traffic services for all member states. Turkey, Switzerland, Austria, Hungary, Malta, and Cyprus are also members of Eurocontrol. But the number of members is growing all the time, and Denmark, Italy and Spain have been accepted for membership, with ratification imminent.

In addition, Eastern European nations have been quick to realise the economic value of air transport to their efforts to open up trade, business and tourism links with the West. Prior to the fall of communism, almost all Eastern Bloc air traffic control was undertaken by Soviet military forces. With the advent of glasnost and the Soviet withdrawal from the former satellite countries, those forces pulled back into the

Below: **The nations that make up the European region of the International Civil Aviation Organisation (ICAO).**
MINISTRY OF TRANSPORT

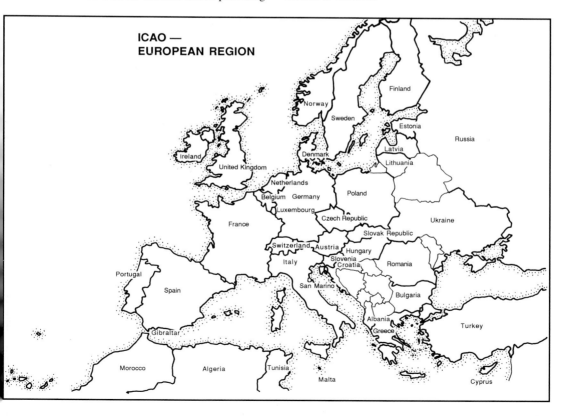

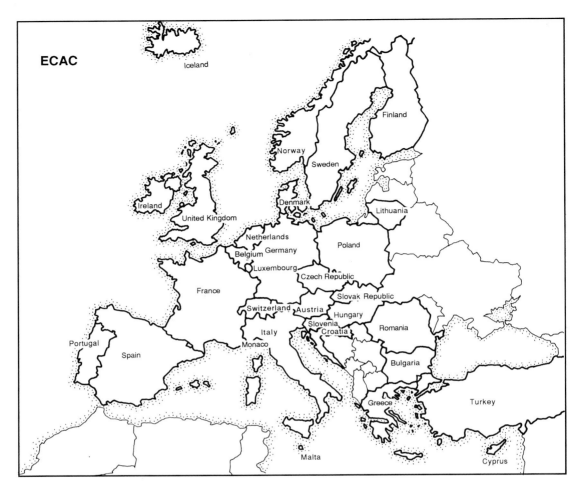

ECAC

Iceland

Finland

Norway

Sweden

Denmark

Lithuania

Ireland

United Kingdom

Netherlands

Poland

Belgium Germany

Luxembourg

Czech Republic

France

Slovak Republic

Switzerland Austria

Hungary

Slovenia

Italy Croatia

Romania

Monaco

Portugal

Spain

Bulgaria

Greece

Turkey

Malta

Cyprus

Soviet Union which subsequently broke up into the Commonwealth of Independent States (CIS) and a number of independent states. The air traffic control system served a predominantly military purpose and was run along military lines. But like the rest of the country it was rapidly running out of funds for repairs, maintenance and upgrades and was becoming obsolete. The situation in the former Soviet Union remains fluid as the constituent parts within both the CIS and the Russian Federation seek greater independence.

In the more far-flung corners of the Eastern Bloc empire, however, the retreating Soviet forces had taken all but the most obsolete equipment with them and also all of the expertise. Because there was no such thing as a civil air traffic control service, there were no civil air traffic controllers and all military control had been provided by the Soviet forces. In addition, what remained of the Soviet government insisted that all new equipment, parts and services must be paid for with hard (foreign) currency, leaving

many of the outlying new republics unable to provide air traffic services.

They were quick to turn to the West for assistance in training controllers and engineers, and for loans or joint venture deals for new equipment. In return, the West endeavoured to ensure that any new systems that were put in place on the fringes of Europe would be compatible with the system that Eurocontrol is working to establish.

All 18 members of Eurocontrol are among the 31 members of the European Civil Aviation Conference (ECAC), an inter-governmental organisation established in 1955 to promote and co-ordinate better utilisation and orderly development of European civil aviation in the economic, technical, security and safety fields. ECAC is urging all its non-Eurocontrol members (Bulgaria, Croatia, the Czech Republic, Finland, Iceland, Lithuania, Monaco, Norway, Poland, Romania, Slovenia, Slovakia and Sweden) to join Eurocontrol as soon as possible.

All ECAC members (except Iceland and Monaco),

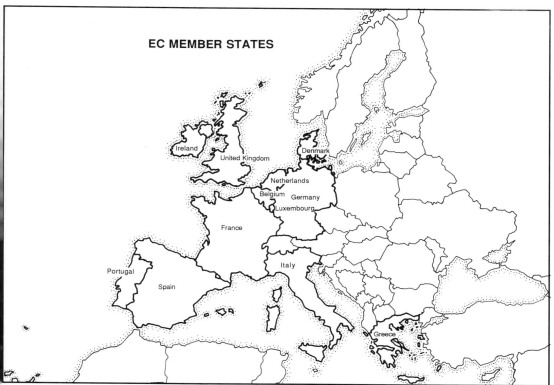

EC MEMBER STATES

Left: **The 31 member states of the European Civil Aviation Conference (ECAC).**
MINISTRY OF TRANSPORT

Above: **The 12 European Community member states.**
MINISTRY OF TRANSPORT

Right: **The various regional organisations which have some input into the creation and operation of a single harmonised and ultimately fully integrated European air traffic control infrastructure.**

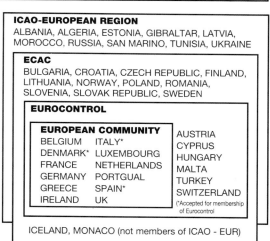

ICAO-EUROPEAN REGION
ALBANIA, ALGERIA, ESTONIA, GIBRALTAR, LATVIA, MOROCCO, RUSSIA, SAN MARINO, TUNISIA, UKRAINE

ECAC
BULGARIA, CROATIA, CZECH REPUBLIC, FINLAND, LITHUANIA, NORWAY, POLAND, ROMANIA, SLOVENIA, SLOVAK REPUBLIC, SWEDEN

EUROCONTROL

EUROPEAN COMMUNITY		
BELGIUM	ITALY*	AUSTRIA
DENMARK*	LUXEMBOURG	CYPRUS
FRANCE	NETHERLANDS	HUNGARY
GERMANY	PORTGUAL	MALTA
GREECE	SPAIN*	TURKEY
IRELAND	UK	SWITZERLAND
		(*Accepted for membership of Eurocontrol)

ICELAND, MONACO (not members of ICAO - EUR)

Eurocontrol, and EC members fall within the jurisdiction of the European division of the International Civil Aviation Organisation (ICAO) which, additionally, covers Albania, Algeria, Estonia, Gibraltar, Latvia, Morocco, Russia, San Marino, Tunisia and the Ukraine and is assumed for aviation purposes to be the definition of European boundaries.

The 31 ECAC member states between them control more than three million square nautical miles of European airspace. This area is roughly equivalent to that of the United States. Within that airspace there are at least 51 air traffic control centres (ATCC) which use 31 different systems incorporating computers from 18 different manufacturers using 22 different operating systems and 33 different programming languages.

The US, by comparison has just 22 fully integrated centres. The entire system is run by the US Federal Aviation Administration (FAA) using common equipment and procedures and all controllers are trained and licensed by a single authority to the same standards.

The result of such historical fragmentation of the European air traffic control network, not surprisingly, is generalised incompatibility and a patchwork of systems which have largely been developed independently. It is this, even more than individual

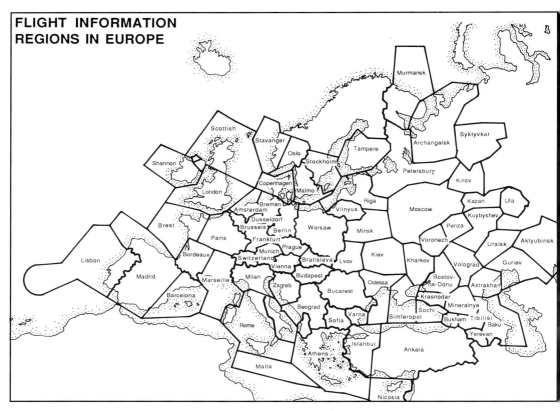

FLIGHT INFORMATION REGIONS IN EUROPE

system deficiencies, which is hampering capacity growth within Europe.

In addition, standards and regulations vary from country to country. Radar separations between aircraft, for example, vary from 5 to 10nm, although in some cases even greater minima are imposed.

Vertical separations between aircraft also vary wildly within ECAC member states: often from ACC (Area Control Centre) to ACC, but sometimes even within an ACC where TMAs and approach zones may have different upper levels. According to ICAO classification, airspace is divided at FL245 into lower airspace (FIR) and upper airspace (UIR), but some states apply a FL195 division or no division at all.

At a meeting in Paris in April 1990, the Transport Ministers of ECAC member states adopted a strategy and action programme for the harmonisation and integration of the operations of their air traffic control systems. It is now more commonly known as EATCHIP (the European Air Traffic Control Harmonisation and Integration Programme), and Eurocontrol was invited to establish the necessary institutional and financial arrangements for the management of the action programme.

The strategy also aims at closer civil/military co-operation, funding Eurocontrol for advanced research, encouraging ECAC member states to join Eurocontrol,

Above: **In the ICAO continental European region alone (excluding North Africa, but including Eastern boundaries of ICAO Europe), air traffic control is highly fragmented, with a total of 74 flight information regions (FIRs).**
CAA

Above right: **Densities of traffic within the ECAC states area in July 1989: the areas surrounding London, Paris and Frankfurt are the busiest.**
ECAC

Right: **The main traffic routes within the ECAC states area in July 1989. Again routes connecting London, Paris, and Frankfurt are the busiest.**
ECAC

and improving the airport/air traffic system interface.

Specific goals include the introduction of a standard *en route* radar separation of five nautical miles for high density areas, and 10nm elsewhere, plus a general review of airspace structure throughout the entire ECAC area.

Having initially agreed that integration was the ultimate solution to the problem, it was realised that this would take some considerable time and an unprecedented level of political co-operation. As a result, the ECAC strategy proposed harmonisation defined by ECAC as 'the attainment of a comparable level of operational system performance throughout a

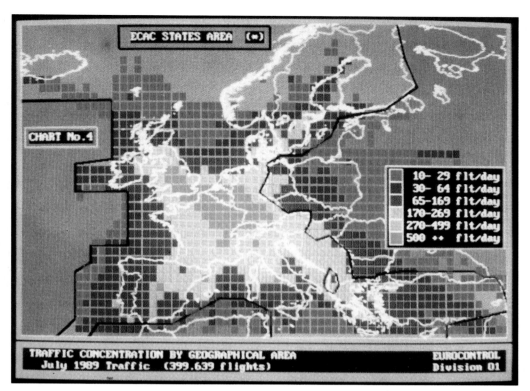

ECAC STATES AREA (*)

CHART No.4

	10- 29 flt/day
	30- 64 flt/day
	65-169 flt/day
	170-269 flt/day
	270-499 flt/day
	500 ++ flt/day

TRAFFIC CONCENTRATION BY GEOGRAPHICAL AREA
July 1989 Traffic (399.639 flights)

EUROCONTROL
Division 01

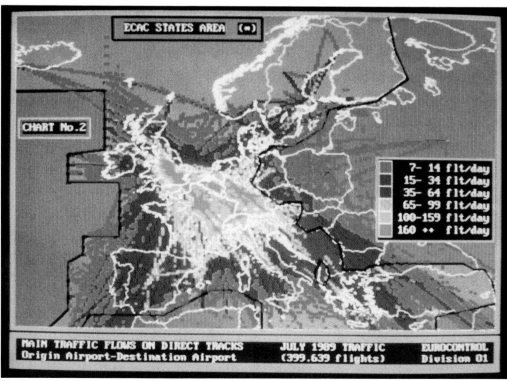

ECAC STATES AREA (*)

CHART No.2

	7- 14 flt/day
	15- 34 flt/day
	35- 64 flt/day
	65- 99 flt/day
	100-159 flt/day
	160 ++ flt/day

MAIN TRAFFIC FLOWS ON DIRECT TRACKS
Origin Airport-Destination Airport

JULY 1989 TRAFFIC
(399.639 flights)

EUROCONTROL
Division 01

given area by utilisation of compatible standards, specifications and procedures' as an interim goal on the way to full integration which ECAC defines as 'the operation of the whole system in a given area in such a manner that, from the user's perspective, it functions as if it were a single unit and that optimum use is made of airspace. Taking account of the existing and developing degree of integration in parts of the area, this can be achieved by applying common standards, specifications and procedures throughout the area, and by common implementation of new systems to attain an identical level of sophistication through use of a common data source.'

EATCHIP

EATCHIP is a four-phase programme stretching over 10 years which should culminate in the creation of a comprehensive European Air Traffic Management System (EATMS).

Its objectives are:
- to optimise the cover and use of radar surveillance through the installation of new radars and wider sharing of existing radar data;
- to improve the efficiency of voice communications and extend data exchange by implementing new equipment and applying common specifications;
- to harmonise the development and implementation of technical ATC systems and sub-systems through the creation of common standards;
- **to improve the management of airspace;**
- to define general guidelines for all human elements of the ATC system.

Specific operational subjects it will be addressing include:
- the optimisation of airspace and route structure, supported by widespread application of area navigation from 1993 onwards;
- full radar coverage throughout the continental ECAC area with the adoption of a standard *en route* separation of five nautical miles in high-density areas (10nm elsewhere) by 1995;
- the progressive integration of all ECAC ATC systems between 1995 and 1998 (harmonisation in high-density areas by 1995 at the latest and elsewhere not later than 1998);
- automatic data exchange between ATC centres by 1998;
- Mode S air/ground datalink from 1998 onwards.

Work on Phase I began in 1990 and was completed the following year. The implementation of Phase IV is scheduled for completion in the year 2000, to provide a working strategy to meet Europe's traffic demand into the next century.

Phase I was the appraisal and evaluation programme which involved incorporating all existing local surveys and analyses of the air traffic control system into a comprehensive in-depth appraisal covering, for the whole of the continental ECAC area, all significant technical characteristics, including airspace and route structure; communications, navigation and surveillance; and the human elements

as they relate to the ATC functions.

Phase II, which was scheduled for completion in late 1993, looks at programme development. This involves:

- detailed planning for medium-term harmonisation and progressive integration, plus the development of specifications and recommendations;
- the development of implementation programmes for specified areas;
- the initial implementation of new route and airspace structures;
- the start of implementation of new facilities and common procedures.

Phase III, which is scheduled for completion between 1995 and 1998, looks at acquisition and implementation, to include:

- the acquisition and installation of new enhanced equipment;

Above: **Eastern European nations have a long way to go to upgrade their systems to compatibility with Western European systems. Poland has installed Westinghouse 20 x 20in high resolution raster scan displays.**
WESTINGHOUSE

Left: **As part of its airspace management system, Poland has installed the Westinghouse ASR-9 airport surveillance radar, pictured here with a Mode S antenna, which can detect air traffic and six levels of weather intensity.**
WESTINGHOUSE

- the continued implementation of new route and airspace structures, plus development of common procedures and system support functions;
- implementation of harmonisation measures throughout the continental ECAC area and progressive integration of air traffic control systems;
- the start of implementation of air/ground datalink facilities;
- the development of proposals to ensure that planning for the continental ECAC area is in line with that of its neighbours.

Phase IV will be implemented between 1995 and 2000 to create the future 'European Air Traffic Management System' (EATMS): an integrated system based on operational requirements and the latest technology. It will be achieved through:

- the adoption of a common functional model integrating the airborne and ground-based components of the future EATMS;
- the definition of transition programmes based on the common model;
- the implementation in specified zones of advanced systems supported by extensive automation and the enhanced data communication available with Mode S satellites and the aeronautical telecommunication network;
- progressive extension of the implementation of advanced systems to other zones.

5. EUROCONTROL

With the fragmented nature of European air traffic services quite clearly restraining airspace capacity, it has long been recognised that the creation of a single authority controlling all of Europe's airspace would be the only way to nurture a coherent, streamlined, efficient and safe system of air traffic control across the continent, within which aircraft would be unconstrained by national boundaries.

The United States has such a system and handles a great deal more traffic than Europe. It has the advantage that all controllers are trained by the same organisation to the same countrywide standards, they follow the same procedures and work with the same equipment whether they are based in New York or Los Angeles. The entire US network is interlinked and since one centre knows exactly what the next is doing, the system is capable of handling greater numbers of aircraft with far fewer bottlenecks. Indeed, it is noticeable that in the US, some 60% of delays are caused by bad weather, with only 35% being ATC-related. (The remaining 5% are usually caused by aircraft or ground equipment failure.) In Europe, conversely, congestion is responsible for almost 80% of all delays, with weather accounting for only 15%.

Similarly, the average delay rate in the US in 1992 was just eight minutes, compared with 21min in Europe.

The European vision stopped just short of total unification in that it related only to the upper airspace, leaving approach and aerodrome control in the hands of the individual sovereign states. It was with that ideal in mind that Eurocontrol was formed. It was set up by an ambitious international convention to plan and execute all air traffic control facilities and operations in the upper airspace of the signatory states, with control centres at Maastricht (the Netherlands), Karlsruhe (Germany), and Shannon (Ireland) plus a training institute in Luxembourg and an experimental centre at Bretigny-sur-Orge near Paris.

However, concerns about national sovereignty were behind the establishment of airspace boundaries in the first place and remain the greatest hindrance to those boundaries coming down. As a result, implementation fell far short of the concept and Eurocontrol has never been allowed to exercise its supra-national authority. Its role in the integration of European air traffic control was temporarily marginalised.

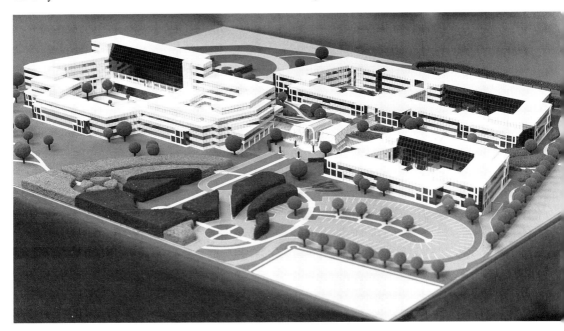

Four States/Eurocontrol Integration Project

In recognition that achievement of any sort of rationalised single European system would be a long-term process, it was decided to develop a model system within which common interfaces were developed between ATCCs so that they could provide an apparently seamless service: ie the users of that integrated airspace would notice no discontinuity and feel that they were being handled by a single authority.

As a result, Eurocontrol began integrating the air traffic control centres of Maastricht, Amsterdam, Brussels, Düsseldorf, and Bremen together with one Dutch, one Belgian, and three German military ATC centres co-located with civil ones. Key to this is the RADNET ('Radar Data Network') programme which gives those centres common and instantaneous access to each other's radar and flight information processing systems.

Although they do not officially form part of the 'Four States Integration Project', four additional civil *en route* centres in Germany — Frankfurt, Karlsruhe, Munich, and Berlin — plus one military centre co-located with Karlsruhe will be incorporated into this network, as will the German and Luxembourg Approach Centres.

Fundamental to this exchange of radar data is the 'Radar Message Conversion and Distribution Equipment' (RMCDE) which is based on a modular microprocessor board system and can adapt and convert radar data to the various interfaces, protocols, formats and line speeds of the different radars connected to the system. Internally, RADNET uses the 'All-Purpose Structured Eurocontrol Radar Information Exchange' (ASTERIX), with conversion between other formats being undertaken through the RMCDEs.

With data supplied by the integrated centres, the Upper Airspace Centre at Maastricht now provides all upper airspace air traffic services for Belgium, Luxembourg, the Netherlands and the northern half of what was formerly West Germany.

Computer links connect neighbouring civil and military units for the automatic exchange of flight plans and radar data. An automatic conflict alert system and many silent co-ordination features assist in the handling of some 700,000 flights each year.

Left: The new Eurocontrol headquarters currently under construction at Haren just outside Brussels in Belgium. Amongst other units, the complex will house the Central Flow Management Unit (CFMU).
EUROCONTROL

CFMU

To ensure the most efficient use of available airspace and thereby optimise capacity, it is essential to manage the traffic flow by regulating the number of flights that are in the system in such a way that no part of the system is overloaded (ie handling more flights than it believes and has declared to be its safe maximum). At the same time, the management system must assure that all available system capacity is used to the maximum extent possible. This process is known as 'Air Traffic Flow Management' (ATFM) and has become an important supplementary service to air traffic control.

ATFM is not new. In the early days of commercial aviation, an airfield which had to close a runway due to either an accident or bad weather would notify its neighbours not to send any additional traffic. It also asked that, when operations could resume, traffic should be staggered until the backlog had caught up. Other airfields would draw up a list of time boxes — or slots — and allocate aircraft registrations to those slots.

The advent of jets and the boom in charter traffic in the early 1960s turned this type of slot allocation — or flow management — from a crisis service into a full congestion tool. Most of the charter traffic was travelling north-south and not all ACCs were able to cope with the sudden increase in traffic in those directions. As a result, those ACCs unable to cope would declare a handling limit, restricting the number of aircraft allowed into their airspace every hour.

The fuel crisis of the early 1970s only heightened the need for ATFM. Until then, airlines departed from their origin airport and were happy to accept a delay upon arrival. It was not unusual for aircraft to hold for up to an hour awaiting landing clearance at their destination. The fuel crisis made airborne holding an expensive luxury that airlines could no longer afford. Potential delays along their route therefore had to be anticipated prior to departure and holding times converted into ground delays before they were given clearance to take off.

In the early 1980s, ICAO's European branch requested Eurocontrol to create a central data bank, known as 'Data Bank Europe' or DBE, to regulate data on air traffic demand for long-term planning purposes. At the same time, 12 national 'Flow Management Units' (FMUs) were established throughout Europe and 'Flow Management Positions' created at ACCs to interface with those FMUs. But like the European system as a whole, it was a fragmented response to a region-wide problem.

Each individual state calculates its own handling capabilities, ie how many aircraft it can safely process within a given period of time. At certain times — for reasons of equipment failure, manpower shortages, strikes, etc — a centre may have to declare a reduced handling capability to ensure that safety is maintained. But few states measure and define capacity in the same way, and some can only estimate what their limit might be. When the capacity of one section of airspace differs greatly from that of its neighbour's on a busy route, a bottleneck develops.

On a typical routeing from London to Athens during the summer, a flight could encounter as many as five restricted areas. The 'Flow Management Unit' in London will calculate, using the aircraft's proposed departure time, the entry time of that aircraft into each of the restricted areas. It will then calculate a departure slot, which is usually a window of 10-20min, which will ensure that the aircraft uses only available slots for passing through any restricted airspace without overloading the system. This may involve a delay on the ground at the originating airport or the operator may be offered an alternative routeing to detour round the bottleneck, but as these are usually longer and less direct, they are therefore more costly and not very popular. What usually happens is that an aircraft will be held at its gate and given a departure clearance only when it is able to proceed along its entire route without overstepping the capacity limitations of any control sector along that route.

This 'flow control' capability is possible in Europe because of the way European airports operate, but it is less so in the United States. There, airlines own or lease their own gates or sections of, or even entire, terminal buildings. If an aircraft belonging to the tenant airline arrives to find all its company gates still occupied, it is not always easy or possible to find alternative facilities. These have to be leased from other carriers at premium short-term rates and the aircraft then fails to link up with its parent systems and services.

It is therefore incumbent upon the airline to ensure that a gate is free to handle arriving aircraft, even if it means forcing a departing aircraft into the take-off sequence long before it is likely to obtain departure clearance. As a result, long lines of aircraft queuing on the taxiways *en route* to the runway are a common sight at many of America's busiest airports: there is much more pressure for an aircraft to move off its stand at the earliest possible opportunity. But this means the aircraft will be holding with its engines running, burning precious fuel and heightening emissions problems.

There is growing pressure for change in the US to rectify this largely inflexible situation. Airports are reviewing the tradition of selling or leasing out terminal assets on a long-term basis because it reduces the airport's flexibility to optimise capacity and cope with last-minute short-term crises. It also leaves the airport particularly vulnerable to airline failures. If a facility has been built specifically for the dedicated use of one airline and that airline folds, the airport is left with an idle facility which is earning no revenue until

it is able to untangle the legal position and find new tenants to reactivate the facility.

In addition, de-icing issues have focused attention on the inappropriateness of pushing back aircraft from the gate even though they may face a significant delay before take off. De-icing fluids are effective for only a limited period of time. If a de-iced aircraft is still queuing to take-off when that effectiveness time limit expires, it is no longer safe to fly and must return to be de-iced for a second time, losing its place in the take-off queue.

In Europe, gates generally belong to the airport and can be assigned as necessary to cope with any given situation. Although an airline may request and traditionally use a specific gate, situations may arise where that particular gate may not be available because the previous occupant is still on stand. An alternative gate will therefore be found for the arriving aircraft. If an aircraft has to be held at the gate because of an ATC delay, the system is sufficiently flexible for an incoming aircraft assigned to that gate to be assigned another even at the last minute and the whole gate allocation process reshaped to accommodate the hiccup.

If an aircraft is unable to utilise the departure slot allocated by the FMU, perhaps because of a technical delay, the controllers will offer that slot — usually at very short notice — to any aircraft able to take it up. Until recently, it was inevitable that national flow management units would allocate slots to national airlines and there was no system for ensuring that all countries and all flights — including air taxis, air ambulances, and private flights — had equal access to an available slot. Because controllers deal with the airlines on a regular basis, know their schedules, and know their level of reliability and ability to expedite a departure, it is inevitable that scheduled airlines tend to get an unfair crack at the whip.

In a bid to overcome this imbalance, Eurocontrol was charged with establishing a 'Central Flow Management Unit' (CFMU) which would co-ordinate slot availability and allocation throughout Europe.

To do this, the number of flow management units around Europe was reduced from 12 to five — London, Paris, Frankfurt, Rome, and Madrid — which would be telephone conferencing linked so that they could act as one body known as 'Central Executive Unit (CEU) West'. A similar service is being established in Eastern Europe and will be known as 'CEU East'.

The five FMUs will progressively transfer their authorities to the Brussels-based CFMU after it becomes operational in 1994. The last FMU to transfer its authority — Madrid — will do so in October 1995.

The CFMU will use the DBE to create at least a basic picture of traffic patterns. This it does using such historical information as regular flight plans and airline schedules to create a picture of at least the planned

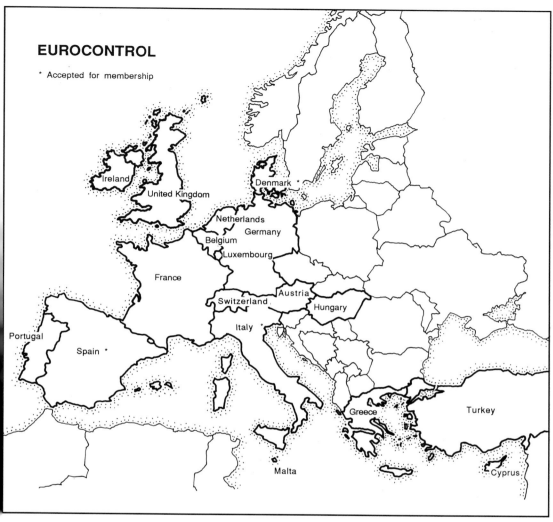

EUROCONTROL

* Accepted for membership

Ireland

United Kingdom

Denmark *

Netherlands

Germany

Belgium

Luxembourg

France

Austria

Switzerland

Hungary

Italy *

Portugal

Spain *

Greece

Turkey

Malta

Cyprus

Above: **The 18 nations which are members of Eurocontrol.**
MINISTRY OF TRANSPORT

scheduled requirements. It does not include military activities nor such *ad hoc* operations as air taxis, air ambulances or private flights, so an adjustment is made to allow a margin for those flights.

At present, all flight plans are sent simultaneously to the five FMUs, the ATC centre nearest the departure point, and all centres along the intended flight path. They are scrutinised by each centre and if there are any errors — unacceptable routes, for example — they have to be manually corrected at each FMU and ATC centre individually; a time consuming and inefficient system.

In future, the CFMU will collect all requests for protection based on declared capacity from all ACCs within Europe and create a detailed list of restrictions. It will also receive all flight plans which it will process, correct if necessary, and distribute immediately to all relevant centres and the operators.

The automation of this process will be made possible by the introduction of a new Integrated Initial Flight Plan Processing System (IFPS). There will be two IFPS centres: one in Brussels at the CFMU and another at Bretigny-sur-Orge. Both will be continuously operational, but will be able to take over the other's responsibilities should problems arise.

The CFMU will be phased in gradually until it is fully operational in 1994, and will be situated in a new purpose-built centre at Haren near Brussels National Airport.

It is likely that, before the end of this century, the CFMU will be managing airspace capacity right across the continent to include much of Eastern Europe.

6. COMMUNICATIONS, NAVIGATION AND SURVEILLANCE

The three key elements of air traffic control are communications, navigation and surveillance (CNS).

Communications involve air-to-ground, ground-to-ground and air-to-air voice and, more recently, data transmissions between controllers and pilots, controllers and other control sectors and between pilots and pilots.

Navigation is the means by which an aircraft travels along a predetermined route to its destination and is directed along that route as necessary by the air traffic controllers on the ground.

Surveillance is a function by which air traffic controllers monitor the movement of aircraft within their particular region of airspace, maintaining the required separations between aircraft and guiding them along their required route.

However, surveillance does not necessarily have to be visual and, indeed where radar is not available, is purely 'procedural' as it is known. Under procedural control, the pilot tells the controller the position, height, and speed of his aircraft, but the controller has no means of visually confirming that position report. If there are a number of aircraft in that sector of airspace, the controller must create a mental picture of the whereabouts, height and direction of all those aircraft and calculate the optimum routeing for each through his sector while ensuring that the aircraft remain a safe distance from each other at all times.

Because the controller cannot visually verify the exact location and track of each aircraft and because he is relying purely on a mental picture of the aircraft movements within his airspace, the separations (lateral distance and height) between aircraft must be greater than if the controller had a visual reference to the traffic in his airspace.

Once radar is brought into play, the controller has a visual reference to all the aircraft operating in his sector. He can therefore provide a visual surveillance service and separations can be reduced accordingly. Lateral separations, for example, vary according to conditions and regions, but range from as much as 60nm with procedural control to as little as 5nm or 10nm under radar surveillance.

The required separations are laid down by ICAO, which is based in Montreal and lays down the international standards and regulations for the whole air transport industry.

Separation requirements vary according to the type of airspace (controlled or uncontrolled), flying conditions (IFR — instrument flight rules — or VFR — visual flight rules), the type of aircraft being flown (wake turbulence or 'jet wash' as it is known from jets can severely upset the stability of smaller aircraft flying behind them), and, in controlled airspace, the handling capability of the air traffic service providers.

A shortage of controllers, lack of automation, or unreliable equipment will quickly impose handling limitations on an air traffic control system.

Following the mid-air collision of two passenger jets over Zagreb, in the former Yugoslavia, in September 1976, resulting in the deaths of 176 passengers and crew, Yugoslavia declared it was no

longer able to handle the same traffic loads and subsequently imposed a strict limit on the number of aircraft that could traverse its airspace at any one time. As Yugoslavian airspace was crossed by most flights from Europe to the Middle and Far East, this restriction often resulted in peak hour bottlenecks. A flight leaving London for Bahrain and Hong Kong, for example, might have been delayed out of London because the number of aircraft expected to be crossing Yugoslavian airspace at the time that aircraft was due to arrive there might already exceed the declared Yugoslavian limit. A departure delay would therefore be built into the flight plan to ensure that the aircraft entered Yugoslavian airspace only as another departed, ensuring that safety limits were strictly observed.

With so many new air routes now open, especially the shorter and therefore highly desirable routes through Russian airspace to the Orient, and airlines tending to favour alternative routes to the Middle East to avoid overflying such occasional trouble spots as Iran and Iraq, Lebanon, and indeed now Yugoslavia itself, the Yugoslavian restrictions no longer pose a problem. But neighbouring states, such as Greece, Italy and Bulgaria, are now having to handle larger numbers of aircraft because of the Yugoslavian conflict.

In Europe as a whole, the level of sophistication in technology used to provide air traffic control services varies substantially from country to country, meaning that some countries have highly sophisticated ATC systems and can handle high densities of traffic while their neighbours have very basic systems, have to maintain wide separation margins and are therefore able to handle far fewer aircraft. This creates bottlenecks in the system and is one of the most common causes of delays in Europe.

It is as much the difference in capability between airspace systems as the density of traffic that causes congestion and the resulting delays, especially in busy regions of the world.

Below: **Concorde on the apron at Larnaca Airport in Cyprus.**

7. AIRPORT CONSTRAINTS

There is, however, a general acceptance that Europe's airspace congestion problems can be solved. The harmonisation and ultimate integration of European ATC systems will enable controllers to make more efficient use of the airspace and cater for larger quantities of traffic.

However, all flights must begin and end at an airport and it is here that capacity problems are significantly more difficult to resolve.

Speaking to delegates at an air traffic control conference, Frederik Sørensen, Chief of Air Transport Policy with the European Commission's Directorate General for Transport (DGVII), said: 'I believe that, to a large extent, it is possible to provide the capacity needed for air traffic control, but it might be more difficult at airports.'

The constraints to European airport growth are entirely environmental and political. Airports are noisy and nobody wants one on their doorstep; those that do have airports close by want to minimise the noise nuisance. Increasing airport traffic is, therefore, unpopular and in Europe lobbies against the development of new airports or the expansion of existing ones are very strong.

Terminal capacity is one factor constraining traffic growth but, in reality, if runway capacity is available, it is usually possible to add terminal space. Terminals in themselves do not generate great quantities of noise and require a relatively compact area of land for development. By their very nature, they will generate additional road traffic and, it stands to reason, air traffic, so there is inevitably resistance to their development, as shown at the moment by the proposals for a fifth terminal at London Heathrow.

But it is runway capacity that is most difficult to add and runways will, once the ATC problems have been solved, be the biggest bottleneck to the system. Runways take up an enormous amount of room. Most major airports handling widebodied intercontinental traffic have runways at least two miles long and between 150 and 200ft wide. In the Middle East, where temperatures are high and lift is therefore reduced, aircraft need much longer take-off runs than they do in colder climates. Most Middle Eastern airports are, therefore, equipped with very long runways — almost three miles in the case of Doha in the Arabian Gulf Emirate of Qatar.

In addition to their length, runways must be as flat as possible and preferably built in line with the prevailing wind of the area so that for most of the time aircraft will be taking off and landing into wind. Runways must also be unobstructed on both sides and at either end. ICAO lays down 'strip width' regulations which determine how much of a buffer margin must be left at either side of the runway to give aircraft on the runway maximum clearance plus a margin for error.

In the Seychelles, for example, if a Boeing 747 is parked at the international terminal, the top of its tail actually intrudes into the buffer zone which means the runway does not meet international strip width minima. However, this is tolerated by ICAO because of the low levels of traffic handled by Seychelles International Airport. In anticipation of further traffic growth, future airport development plans will address this problem.

Wellington Airport in New Zealand has a similar problem, with houses so close to the runway that it is not possible to meet strip width requirements. Because Wellington is so tightly land constrained, it also operates with strip width exemptions.

The approaches to either end of the runway must also be unobstructed by hills, buildings or other tall structures. Most aircraft make an average 3° descent to land and need to be assured of a wide margin of terrain clearance. Similarly, a heavily laden aircraft on take-off needs a clear climb out run, without having to make sharp turns or other manoeuvres to avoid obstacles in its path.

Many of today's ground-based radio navigation aids also need to be unobstructed by terrain or structures in order to operate accurately and efficiently. So in addition to the runway itself, there needs to be a large buffer zone around it. Runways can be and are built without meeting the full range of international requirements, but these are usually in difficult locations, such as Kathmandu and other mountainous regions or areas riddled by fjords and lakes, where it is impossible to provide the safety margins required of larger airports. However, these airports are usually handling relatively low levels of traffic.

Because of all these specialist requirements, runways are extremely costly to build and construction takes several years.

But, undoubtedly, the biggest constraint to runway development is pressure against noise. Runways generate more noise than any other part of an airport because aircraft are operating at high power settings when they are using the runway — either employing

Above: **A busy day at Amsterdam's Schiphol Airport. Capacity on the ground needs to match growth in the air.**
AMSTERDAM AIRPORT SCHIPHOL

ull thrust for take-off or reverse thrust for landing. There is always strong resistance to the addition of unways at any airport in Europe. In a bid to appease environmental lobbyists, the new Munich airport has had to build its runways long enough — 4,000m — that aircraft can land and roll to a stop without having to employ reverse thrust, thereby reducing the noise nuisance.

Given that the addition of extra runways almost anywhere in Europe is, at best, going to be an extremely difficult battle, it seems that runways will ultimately be the biggest constraint to traffic growth within the region. A great deal of effort is being put in to maximising existing capacity and this certainly seems to be relatively successful. London Heathrow, for example, has had the same two-runway configuration since the airport opened for commercial operation in 1946. (It does have a third, crosswind runway, but this is used only when wind conditions are such that it is impossible to operate on the two main runways.) Then, it was handling 2,046 aircraft movements a year. Since then the runways have been lengthened, strengthened and widened to handle jets and widebodied aircraft, with the last major extension completed as long ago as 1967. Today, those same two runways are handling close to 400,000 movements a year.

And now BAA plc, which owns and operates the three London airports — Heathrow, Gatwick and Stansted — is planning to build a fifth terminal at Heathrow to handle an additional 30 million passengers a year, bringing the airport's passenger handling capability up to 80 million passengers a year, without adding any additional runway capacity. This has been achieved through ever more efficient use of the runways, spreading peaks where possible, and by the airlines using larger aircraft, carrying more passengers per aircraft movement.

However, there comes a point when it is no longer possible safely to tweak runway capacities up any further. All the aircraft being channelled into the precision approach system must land on the same runway and it is becoming impossible at the most congested airports to reduce further separation between landing and departing aircraft.

Add some bad weather, which reduces visibility, and an airport's capacity to handle arriving and departing aircraft suddenly plummets. Precision approach systems can bring aircraft safely in to land, but once he is on the ground, the pilot is on his own. If the visibility on the ground is too poor for the controllers in the tower to be able to see the aircraft and guide it safely to the terminal, it will not be given permission to land.

ICAO has defined a series of operational criteria for runways which determine the conditions under which aircraft may land or take off.

The most basic is a non-instrument runway which can be used only for visual approaches. An instrument runway provides some form of non-visual guidance, but this is usually relatively imprecise and does not provide a rate of descent reference.

Precision approaches are broken down into three categories which take into account the sophistication, reliability and integrity of the equipment at the airport,

the runway lighting, the prevalent weather conditions, and the level of sophistication and duplication of the equipment on board the aircraft.

- Category I denotes a minimum cloud base/decision height (if the pilot cannot see the runway at this point, he must abandon the approach and initiate a 'go-around') of 200ft with forward visibility on the runway no less than 2,600ft.
- Category II denotes a cloud base/decision height of no more than 100ft, with a visibility of 1,200ft.
- Category III is for 'blind landings' when there is no cloud base and therefore no decision height. This category is further broken down into three subdivisions: Cat IIIA requiring a minimum runway visibility of 750ft, Cat IIIB requiring a minimum runway visibility of just 150ft, and Cat IIIC which requires no visual reference at all.

The ability to use those categories of runway depends on the aircraft being flown. If the aircraft is only equipped to Cat II, but Cat III conditions exist, the aircraft cannot land. Likewise if the runway is only Cat II equipped and an aircraft is Cat III equipped, it

Below: **Land constraints mean that Wellington Airport in New Zealand has to have special dispensation to operate at less than the ICAO strip width minima. The nearest house is less than 150m from the runway centreline. This picture is taken from the air traffic control tower which is set on a hill two streets away from the airport perimeter in the middle of a residential area.**

can only land on that runway if the cloud base is no less than 100ft and runway visibility is 1,200ft or greater.

Only about 25% of the world's major airports are equipped for Cat III operations, and most of these are in Europe and the United States — not altogether surprisingly since these regions are prone to the bad weather that makes precision approaches an operational necessity if airports are not to close for much of the winter.

Once the aircraft is on the ground, it is the tower controller's responsibility to direct it safely to its parking gate. If that aircraft were the only one operating at a particular airport, the controller's job would be simple even if he could not see that aircraft. But at busy international airports, aircraft are always on the move, taxiing in from a flight, or out for a departure, or over to a maintenance hangar, or just away from the terminal to a long-term parking bay. In addition, there are hordes of ground vehicles constantly moving round an airport. In conditions of poor visibility, such as a thick fog, ensuring that there are no collisions on the ground is a problem that has yet to be fully addressed.

Although a controller may direct an aircraft along a specific route, that aircraft may in the haze get seriously lost and could stray into the path of another aircraft, or even on to an active runway. The worst case of this was when two Boeing 747s collided on the runway at Tenerife airport in the Canary Isles in 1977 in thick fog. It remains the worst accident in aviation history and highlighted the very real problem of ground control in reduced visibility.

There are two means of controlling movements on the ground at airports: lighting and ground movement radar. Lighting controls vary enormously from airport to airport, but the main elements include green 'follow me' taxiway centreline lights to guide the aircraft along a designated route, flashing amber 'wig wag' lights at critical junctions, and the use of a row of red lights known as a 'stopbar' — which aircraft may not cross as long as it is illuminated— at every entry point to the runway. When an aircraft waiting at a stopbar is given clearance to move on to the runway, the controller switches off the red lights and the aircraft is free to proceed.

Ground movement radar is essentially a primary radar *(see Tools of ATC)* that picks up echoes from any targets on the airfield. It also picks up a great deal of other airport clutter, but these systems are being increasingly refined to offer greater resolution.

Its greatest disadvantage is that it is not able to offer a positive identification of targets and until it does, controllers will be unable to use it as a failsafe control tool in conditions of reduced visibility. A number of labelling technologies are currently under study and it should not be long before this problem is solved so that controllers will be able to provide a positive ground control service.

8. TOOLS OF ATC

The tools used for communications, navigation and surveillance all involve the use of radio transmissions and are, therefore, range-restricted. In the case of systems that operate in the higher frequency bands, they are also constrained by the 'line-of-sight' rule. That is, that the characteristics of radio waves are such that they normally travel in a straight line unless they are 'bent' by atmospheric phenomena, reflected by dense objects, or screened by high terrain. In most cases, therefore, it also follows that the greater the height of the aircraft, the greater the range of navigation aids being used.

RADIO AIDS TO SURVEILLANCE

Radar

'Radio Detection and Ranging', more commonly known as 'Radar', introduces the visual surveillance factor into air traffic control. It is the means by which controllers can obtain a visual reference to all aircraft within their sector and separations can accordingly be reduced.

Radar was invented during World War 2 and was subsequently adopted by the budding civil air transport sector as a key air traffic control tool. Then, and for a

Left: **A Thomson-CSF RSM 970 Monopulse Secondary Surveillance Radar (MSSR) at Palaiseau in France.**
THOMSON-CSF

Above: **An RSM 970 MSSR associated to a TRAC 2000 solid state approach radar at Hawkins Hill, Wellington, New Zealand.**
THOMSON-CSF

Right: **The Athens approach radar station.**
THOMSON-CSF

long time afterwards, traffic was monitored using data generated by primary radar. This works by transmitting concentrated pulses of radio energy which reflect off any dense objects in their path to produce an echo. As soon as a pulse encounters an object — be it a mountain, an aircraft, or even a very dense weather system — the beam is reflected back to the radar sensor which calculates the range of the obstacle by measuring the amount of time (at the speed of light) that it takes for the radio wave to go out to an object and then return to the receiving antenna.

All obstacles encountered during each circular sweep of the radar sensor are displayed on a radar screen as a 'blip' or target.

Because radio waves usually travel in a straight line, they cannot detour round obstacles which curtail their line of travel: radar — like all other radio-based systems

Above: A Swissair MD-80 taxying past the domed primary radar site and control tower at Milan's Linate airport.
ALENIA

Left: An experimental Mode S station has been tested at Paris's Orly Airport. For aircraft which are not Mode S equipped, the radar acts as a standard Monopulse Secondary Surveillance Radar (MSSR).
THOMSON-CSF

Below: The distinctive Alenia ALE 3 x 5 primary radar has a multi-beam array for better coverage. This is the installation at Milan's Linate Airport.

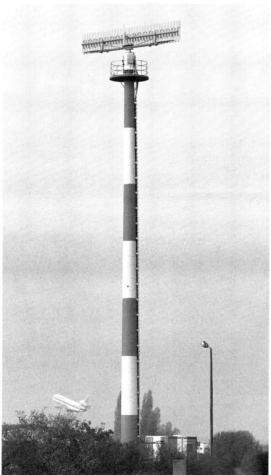

Top: **An Alitalia DC-9 takes off past the control tower and dome-protected secondary surveillance radar at Rome's Fiumicino Airport.**

Above: **Secondary surveillance radar with a protective dome. Milan/Linate Airport.**

— is therefore a 'line-of-sight' instrument and vulnerable to screening by mountains or even — if the aircraft is flying low enough — by the earth's curvature.

An aircraft flying behind a mountain, for example, would not be visible to radar, but as soon as it climbed above the mountain or emerged from behind it, the aircraft would once again appear as a target on the radar screen. The higher the aircraft, the greater the radar range. In mountainous regions it is, therefore, difficult to provide low level radar coverage which is why airports like Kathmandu in Nepal, which are difficult to fly into even under the best conditions, cannot be made safer with the introduction of radar or indeed other line-of-sight navigational aids.

The biggest drawback with primary radar is that it can only highlight targets within its range: it cannot positively identify those targets or their altitude. The controller must paint a three-dimensional picture in his mind so that he knows the identification of each target, its altitude (as reported by the pilot), where it is going, how fast it is going and whether it is likely to conflict with any of the other targets on the screen.

Left: The new area control centre in Istanbul, Turkey, which is a member of ICAO Europe.

Below: A Mode S large vertical aperture secondary radar antenna.
COSSOR/RAYTHEON

Right: A Lufthansa jet takes off past the monopulse secondary surveillance and approach radars at Vienna Airport in Austria.
THOMSON-CSF

If in doubt about a particular target's identity, the controller can request that aircraft to undertake a specific manoeuvre, such as a turn off course followed by a return to course. By watching which target on his screen makes a momentary detour from course, the controller can pinpoint exactly which aircraft it is. It is a system that works well in areas of low traffic density. In busy skies, however, the controller is faced with a screen crowded with one dimensional targets for which he is trying to provide a three dimensional air traffic control service. Under those conditions, identifying manoeuvres becomes more hazardous and some form of positive target identification is essential.

The answer is secondary radar. Unlike primary radar which does not require the aircraft to carry any response equipment, secondary radar is an interrogative system: it transmits a signal to the aircraft, to which the aircraft replies with a coded transmission. The aircraft must therefore be equipped with response equipment, known as a transponder.

In order to identify a particular target, the ground controller will ask that aircraft to transpond or 'squawk' an assigned code number which immediately highlights a target on the controller's screen,

identifying it as that particular aircraft. If the aircraft is equipped with what is known as a Mode C transponder, the altitude of that aircraft will also be displayed in the identifying label on screen. If the aircraft is not equipped with a transponder, it will not register on the controller's radar screen at all unless a primary radar is also feeding data to that screen — in which case, the aircraft will appear as an unidentified target.

These days, most radar data is collected in a computer processing system which extracts the relevant aircraft information and discards the clutter of echoes generated by terrain or weather to create a much cleaner radar display showing all targets and, where relevant, identifying labels.

In busy airspace, or in the vicinity of terminal areas, primary and secondary radar sensors are generally mounted together to ensure that controllers are aware not only of all transponder-equipped aircraft in their sector, but also any traffic operating without transponders. For upper level *en route* surveillance, longer range secondary surveillance radar is generally used alone because there is less traffic density and few, if any, aircraft operate in those sectors without transponders.

Top: **The DVOR/DME at Marseille in France.**
THOMSON-CSF

Above: **The DVOR at Goodwood.**
RACAL AVIONICS

Like its primary counterpart, secondary radar is a line-of-sight tool and range-restricted.

Where full secondary radar coverage is available, it is possible to reduce the separations required between aircraft and, therefore, make more efficient use of the available airspace, thereby increasing the capacity of that controlled airspace.

However, radar is limited to a range of about 200nm. On land, it is usually possible to install a sufficient number of radar sites to provide full radar coverage, particularly as aircraft climb away from the earth's surface and obstacle interference. But it is impossible to provide radar cover over the full expanse of the world's oceans and it is rarely viable to provide full cover in the depths of inaccessible terrain such as vast deserts.

Multi-radar tracking

These days, in many busy areas, radar coverage is so comprehensive that several radar returns are generated for each aircraft. In reality, radar bias (the radar signal may be weakened by distance, weather conditions or other interference) or systematic error between radars means that each radar will give a slightly different position reading. The radar data processor will, therefore, select the reading from the radar providing the strongest signal and translate that into a target on the air traffic control display.

Today, multi-radar trackers collate the signal data from all the relevant radars, calculate the strength of each return, and using all this information, define the aircraft's precise position.

Precision Approach Radar

At airports where it is not possible to install an 'Instrument Landing System' or ILS (see Radio aids to Navigation), but it may be necessary to offer a precision approach capability, ICAO recommends the use of 'Precision Approach Radar' (PAR). In these circumstances, a local controller literally talks the aircraft down on to the runway. Because it is

expensive and rarely used, PAR is not widely applied.

It involves the use of two radar pictures, giving the controller both azimuth and elevation views of the aircraft on approach. The controller will then talk to the pilot, giving minute navigation instructions to get the aircraft established on the centreline and glideslope and keep it there for the entire descent. In order for the controller to give accurate instructions, he must have the elevation/height information included in the display. A straightforward azimuth or plan display would provide insufficient data.

Mode S

'Mode Select', or 'Mode S' as it is more commonly known, is a system which enhances existing radar-

Below: **Controllers use ground movement radar to monitor the movement of aircraft and other vehicles on the ground, especially when bad weather reduces visibility and the controller is unable to see the whereabouts of aircraft on the airport. Zurich Airport.** SIEMENS PLESSEY SYSTEMS

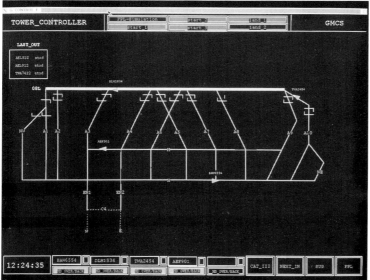

Above: **Ground movement radar in the Gatwick control tower helps maintain safe separations between aircraft on the ground when darkness or bad weather limits the controller's ability to see the aircraft as they taxi off the runway and into the terminal area.**
RACAL AVIONICS

Left: **Ground movement control systems are generally based on primary radar data, but presentation of that data on screen is becoming increasingly sophisticated. Here, the yellow arrows represent aircraft and show in which direction the aircraft is travelling. In the event of a potential conflict, the relevant arrows will turn red and an alert issued to the controller.**
SIEMENS

Above right: **The ground movement radar atop the control tower at Zurich Airport.**
SIEMENS PLESSEY SYSTEMS

based surveillance and provides an additional datalink function. It has been developed in order to overcome sensitivity of existing systems to synchronous garble and a critical shortage of transponder codes. Existing systems are unable to assign unique identity codes to more than 4,096 aircraft in any one region at any given time. Although all aircraft operating in a specified region have individual codes, those same codes have to be used by other aircraft operating in different regions across the globe. An aircraft passing through

several regions may therefore have to be assigned a new identity code as it passes from one region into another to avoid an identity conflict with an aircraft already operating in that region with the same code.

Mode S, however, is capable of recognising up to 16 million unique codes which means that every aircraft currently in existence could be assigned its own unique code when the Mode S transponder is installed. This code cannot be changed from the cockpit. Mode S codes are derived from the aircraft's

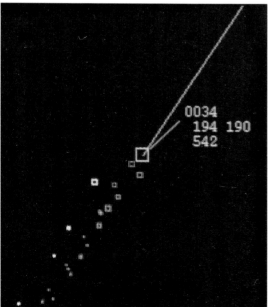

Left: Multi radar tracking incorporates the use of data from a number of radar sensors. For various geographic or meteorological reasons, radar bias or systematic error between radars means that each return will place the aircraft in a slightly different position (the small blips pictured). Traditional multi radar tracking technology extracts the strongest radar signal and displays that on the controller's screen. Today's new systems actually calculate the accuracy of each return according to each sensor's position and bias perimeters and represent an accurate picture of the aircraft's position (the large, labelled target).
NOBELTECH SYSTEMS AB

registration number or other numbering scheme.

Another key feature of Mode S is that it can selectively interrogate individual aircraft even if several transponder-equipped aircraft are simultaneously within view of the ground sensor. A Mode S transponder will not respond to a 'roll call' interrogation that is not specifically addressed to that transponder. However, in order to pick up unknown aircraft, a sensor periodically broadcasts a Mode S 'all-call' interrogation. Any Mode S transponder which has not been specifically commanded to ignore all-call interrogations will reply. Once a transponder has responded to an all-call interrogation and been

Above: **Radar displays have evolved from the early horizontal Plan Position Indicator round screens to the most up to date Sony 2000 line x 2000 pixel full colour, vertical raster screens.**
THOMSON-CSF

Right: **The new full-colour raster display screens offer much higher definition than older technology. This screen configuration includes computerised flight plans.**

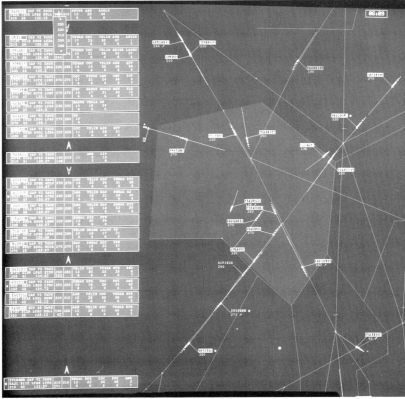

identified, the sensor will then instruct it to ignore all further all-call interrogations. Mode S is claimed to improve overall surveillance accuracy by a factor of up to four.

As a datalink tool, Mode S uses the basic surveillance interrogations and replies to pass datalink messages, taking advantage of the selective address to exchange more comprehensive data. As a result, air traffic controllers can receive on screen more information about the status of each aircraft interrogated than is currently possible with Mode A (identity) and Mode C (altitude).

In addition, using the Mode S datalink function, a pilot may access weather and flight information services, flight safety services, Automated Terminal Information Services (ATIS), initial connection services, and automated *en route* air traffic control connection mode services.

Mode S has been adopted by ICAO as the Secondary Surveillance Radar (SSR) standard of the future.

Displays

Display technology has made great strides over the last few years, giving controllers a much clearer picture of the airspace they are controlling.

From the early days of round horizontal monochrome displays, air traffic control authorities are increasingly switching to vertical square colour screens.

Until the advent of SSR, all radar surveillance involved the use of primary sensors. The data generated by these sensors was displayed on round PPI ('Plan Position Indicator') screens with a beam making a circular scan of the screen to represent each revolution of the radar antenna, updating the echos with every revolution. But, as well as picking up aircraft, the screen also displayed all other echoes generated by the radar and, as a result, the picture received by the controller was often cluttered.

The advent of SSR and the use of transponders meant that it was at last possible positively to identify and label targets and, as display technology improved, to select the amount of additional information that was displayed on the screen. It was possible, for example, to screen out terrain and weather echoes, leaving just the active targets and giving controllers a much clearer picture.

Today, almost all displays are in fact synthetic pictures created from data generated by both primary and secondary surveillance radar. The information is received at the radar data processor which filters out any unwanted information and presents the aircraft targets on the controller's screen, with an identity tag if the information is generated by a transponder, or as an untagged target if no transponder is present. In busy and terminal airspace, both primary and secondary surveillance radars are used to ensure that any traffic operating without a transponder is picked up on the screen and not causing a hazard to other traffic.

Another development is the increasing use of raster displays to replace the more conventional PPI. Raster technology is used in television screens, but in its ATC application, involves a much higher number of lines and pixels to provide greater resolution. Raster screens are more commonly square than round and refresh in a horizontal rather than circular format. The most widely adopted raster ATC display currently available is a 2,000 line x 2,000 pixel 20sq in screen developed by Sony of Japan, although smaller screens are available that offer ever greater resolution.

For the on-screen image, more use is being made of windows software, and the use of colour is providing further safety enhancements, although definitive regulations governing the use of colour are still being finalised. Eurocontrol is devoting a considerable amount of R&D resources to the creation of a universal colour screen format to be adopted as the standard throughout Europe in the harmonisation and integration programme.

The use of colour, new screen technology, and ongoing research into the development of non-reflective glass has also meant that controllers are at last able to come out of the dark. For optimum definition, radar controllers have always worked in darkened rooms where discreet lighting has had to be carefully positioned to ensure no reflections corrupted the screen picture. Now controllers can work in natural daylight, although direct sunlight or the sort of brightness found in control towers can severely degrade resolution.

RADIO AIDS TO NAVIGATION

There are a number of ground-based radio aids which, together with the airborne 'Inertial Navigation System' (INS), make up the navigation part of air traffic control. They vary widely in sophistication and use, but the following are the most widely adopted navaids.

NDB

The 'Non-Directional Beacon' (NDB) is one of the most simple forms of radio navigation aid. It is a radio transmitter that emits a continuous signal on a published frequency, and can be positively identified by a morse code signal that it emits at frequent intervals. It offers no tracking guidance and most aircraft are fitted with an 'Automatic Direction Finder' (ADF) to identify the direction of the beacon from the aircraft.

Operating in low frequency bands (200-800kHz), NDBs are subject to interference from bad weather, coastal refraction, and ionospheric activity at night. However, because low and medium frequency signals follow the curvature of the earth (diffraction), NDBs are not bound by the line-of-sight rule. Therefore, if an aircraft is within the power range of the beacon,

transmissions can be received regardless of the altitude of the aircraft. NDBs are usually used in the vicinity of airports as an aid to locating the airport itself.

VOR

The 'Very High Frequency (VHF) Omni-directional Radio Range' (VOR) is a much more sophisticated navaid, used as a guidance along airways, for centre-line guidance, and often as a reporting point. The VOR beacon transmits a continuous signal in a radial pattern through 360°, producing 360 separate tracks or radials that can be used by the pilot to fly to or from the VOR.

In the aircraft, the pilot receives a visual indication of the direction of the beacon and can therefore ascertain which radial he is crossing and his position in relation to that beacon. If required, he can also determine his position relative to a selected radial.

Because VOR operates in the very high frequency (108-117.95MHz) bands it is not subject to atmospheric disturbances, but it is subject to line-of-sight constraints. The higher the aircraft, the greater the range of the VOR, but the VOR's accuracy also deteriorates with distance.

VOR accuracy can be enhanced with the addition of Doppler (DVOR) by which fluctuations in

frequency wave motion emitted by an object moving at speed can be calculated. DVORs are being increasingly installed around the globe instead of, or in conjunction with, standard VORs.

DME

'Distance Measuring Equipment' (DME) is normally co-located with a VOR. While the VOR gives bearing information in relation to that beacon, the DME provides information about the aircraft's distance from the beacon, giving a much more precise position indicator to the pilot.

DME acts as an airborne secondary radar. An airborne interrogator sends out coded paired pulses of radio energy at specific spacing, which are received by the ground station. This triggers a ground transponder to send out a reply pulse at the same pulse spacing but on a different frequency. Computers in the aircraft measure the amount of time it takes from initial transmission of a pulse from the aircraft until the reply signal is received, and translate that into the distance (usually in nautical miles) of the aircraft from the beacon. It actually measures the slant distance rather than the ground distance, which is in fact slightly longer, but not enough to seriously affect accuracy. The DME is least accurate when the aircraft is

Above left: **Although still widely used in ATC sites all over Europe and the world, the circular monochrome screens, seen here at Frankfurt, are increasingly being replaced with ....**
DFS

Above: **....the 20sq in high resolution colour displays pictured here during trials for CCF application at LATCC.**
SIEMENS PLESSEY SYSTEMS

Right: **The 'windows' concept gives controllers more immediate access to a greater range of information on screen. A standardised format for Europe and regulations regarding the use of colour have yet to be finalised.**
GEC-MARCONI

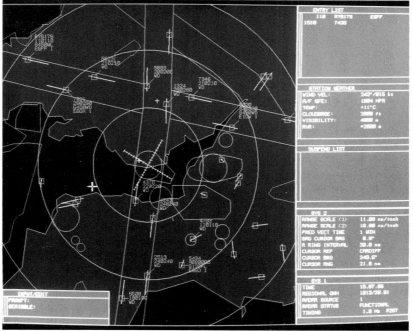

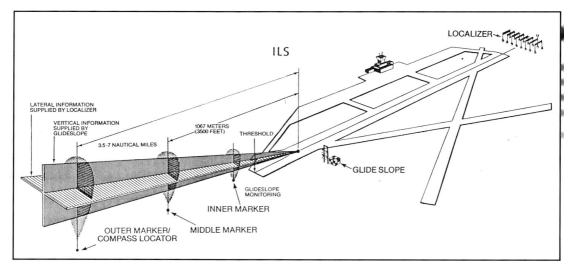

LATERAL INFORMATION
SUPPLIED BY LOCALIZER

VERTICAL INFORMATION
SUPPLIED BY
GLIDESLOPE

3.5-7 NAUTICAL MILES

1067 METERS
(3500 FEET)

THRESHOLD

ILS

LOCALIZER

GLIDE SLOPE

GLIDESLOPE
MONITORING

INNER MARKER

MIDDLE MARKER

OUTER MARKER/
COMPASS LOCATOR

overhead the beacon because it will measure the height of the aircraft from the beacon and translate that into distance.

DME operates in the Ultra High Frequency (UHF) spectrum between 962MHz and 1,213MHz.

PRECISION APPROACH SYSTEMS

ILS

At present, the standard precision approach tool is the 'Instrument Landing System' (ILS). It incorporates two basic elements: a localiser beam which guides the aircraft on to the runway centreline, and a glideslope which indicates the angle of approach that should be maintained to bring the aircraft over the runway threshold at the required height. Both elements transmit radio beams angled so that if the aircraft is not on the centreline, either laterally or vertically, there is a modulation deviation which translates in the cockpit as a deviation off course and tells the pilot which way to turn to recapture the correct signal.

The localiser antenna is a fence-like structure located at right angles to the runway about 1,000ft off the far end. It transmits two overlapping 'lobes' of radio energy which are transmitted horizontally on the same VHF frequency. The carrier waves of the two lobes are modulated at different frequencies, and the centreline is defined by the point where the two lobes overlap. If the aircraft is off centre, the modulation deviation is detected and the necessary correction shown on the flight instrument display.

The glideslope uses two similarly overlapping lobes of radio energy, but these are transmitted vertically on the same UHF frequency with differing modulation. Other than that, it operates in much the same way as the localiser, telling the pilot if the aircraft is too high or too low.

The ILS is usually calibrated to 10 miles out, but

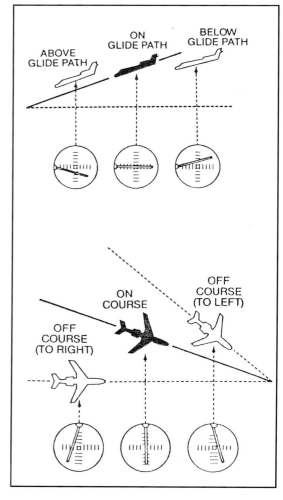

ABOVE
GLIDE PATH

ON
GLIDE PATH

BELOW
GLIDE PATH

ON
COURSE

OFF
COURSE
(TO LEFT)

OFF
COURSE
(TO RIGHT)

Left: The Instrument Landing System (ILS) has long been the standard precision approach aid. It guides the aircraft on to the runway by transmitting a localiser (centreline) beam and a glidescope (rate of descent) beam. For an accurate approach, the aircraft needs to have captured the point at which the horizontal and vertical beams intersect.

Below left: The pilot has instruments on the flightdeck which indicate if the aircraft is above or below the glideslope, and left or right of the centreline. By following the direction that the needle is pointing, the aircraft will recapture the ILS.

Below: The ILS beam consists of two radio beams generated by two separate transmitters located along the runway. They come in a variety of shapes and sizes, but the glide slope transmitter is usually a tall radio mast-like structure located near the touchdown area and up to 600 feet from the centreline off to one side of the runway.
SIEMENS PLESSEY SYSTEMS

Right: The localiser antenna is a fence-like structure set at right angles to the runway and about 1,000ft off the end of it.
SIEMENS PLESSEY SYSTEMS

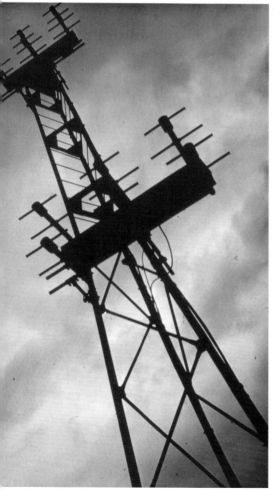

Above: ILS transmitters come in a variety of shapes and sizes. This Racal Avionics Category III system has been installed at Luton and East Midlands airports in the UK.

can be picked up and locked on as far as 25 or even 50 miles out. Marker beacons are positioned along the ILS, within the last few miles before touchdown, transmitting low-power fan-shaped signals which can be received only by an aircraft passing directly above the antenna. The outer marker (OM) is usually sited about five nautical miles from the runway threshold and is often positioned with a locator NDB. The

Above: **A British Airways Boeing 747-200 taxies behind one of the ILS localiser antennas at Heathrow.**
THOMSON-CSF

Below: **A Boeing 747 descends over the ILS localiser antenna at Luton Airport.**
RACAL AVIONICS

middle marker (MM) is usually located about half a mile from the runway, and an inner marker (IM) may be located at the threshold, but with the approach speeds of today's jet aircraft, this inner marker is all but obsolete, although it may — on a Cat II approach for example — represent decision height.

The beacons all transmit on the same frequency, but each transmits its own morse code identifier. The markers are also visually identified on the flight deck: the OM as a flashing blue light, the MM as a flashing amber light, and the IM — if there is one — by a flashing white light.

The ILS is a much tried and tested system and has served the industry well for many years, but it does have some drawbacks.

Because it uses the ground in front of the glideslope antenna to form the beam, a large area in front of this antenna must be level. The cost of site preparation can sometimes exceed the purchase cost of the equipment, making it site-sensitive and expensive to install.

In addition, the glideslope is sensitive to reflective surfaces so the path of the beam must be kept free of obstructions for much of its operational length. Its application is therefore limited in areas of rough terrain, mountains, or large man-made structures. In addition, this can affect surface movements at the airport because taxying aircraft must be held well clear of the glideslope transmitter. This may reduce the movement handling capacity of the airport.

In its standard airport configuration, ILS also provides only a single, narrow approach path and is not flexible enough to handle the high-angle approaches used by STOL (short take-off and landing) aircraft or helicopters. However, in specific environments this problem can be solved and London City Airport was the first to install an ILS with a steep 7.5° glideslope angle, compared with the usual 3° to 3.5° ILS glideslope. Plymouth City Airport also operates a customised system and operates an ILS which can switch from a 3.5° glideslope to 7.5° to meet the differing needs of the aircraft types using the facility.

But perhaps the most critical problem facing the continued use of ILS is that there are only 40 ILS channels available and frequency congestion is

Below: **A special ILS was designed for installation at London City Airport to facilitate the unusually steep approach angle required for landing on the city centre runway in London's Docklands.** LONDON CITY AIRPORT

becoming a serious problem in some regions, particularly in parts of the United States and Europe. With much wider demand for access to VHF frequencies from popular radio broadcasters, there is little opportunity for increasing the number of ILS channels available. Interference on ILS frequencies in congested areas can corrupt the signal and it is becoming increasingly difficult to add ILS facilities in areas where this is happening.

MLS

As a result, much time and effort has been dedicated to finding an alternative precision approach system, with the result that the 'Microwave Landing System' (MLS) has been selected as the precision approach tool to take the industry into the next century.

MLS, which operates at frequencies of about 5,000MHz, emits two fan-shaped microwave beams which sweep laterally and vertically, providing an azimuth (the MLS equivalent of the ILS localiser) beam, and an elevation (equivalent to the ILS glideslope) beam. But rather than transmitting a steady beam, the MLS azimuth beam makes an 80° — or, at some locations, 120° — sweep covering an area of 40° (or 60°) either side of the runway centreline, while the elevation beam covers an area from 0.9° to 15° (most aircraft make a 3° approach so this provides ample redundant coverage). The MLS is usually used in conjunction with precision DME (DME/P) to give greater accuracy of range information. DME/P has an accuracy of plus or minus 100ft in the final approach mode, compared to plus or minus 600ft in the standard DME.

During each complete scanning cycle, each of the MLS beams sweep across its fan-shaped coverage area and then back, with a brief pause after each full scanning cycle. When an aircraft enters the MLS range, an onboard receiver can detect which is a 'to' pulse and which is a 'from' pulse. By measuring the amount of time it takes each pulse to travel to the edge of the coverage area and return to the target, the aircraft receiver can calculate its precise position within the azimuth and elevation beams.

The advantage is that, rather than needing to capture a single centreline beam, an aircraft can enter the MLS coverage area anywhere within the 80° (or 120°) sweep and be given a precise guide to the runway centreline, known as a curved approach. It would therefore be possible to install MLS at airports where obstructions make it impossible to have an ILS approach. Even if the direct centreline were obstructed, aircraft could still make curved precision approaches and capture the actual centreline much later in the approach. In reality, however, controllers at

Left: The Microwave Landing System (MLS) azimuth transmitter at London Heathrow. Behind that can be seen the fence-like structure of the ILS localiser beacon.
SIEMENS PLESSEY SYSTEMS

Right: Testing is now under way on Microwave Landing Systems (MLS) which are due to replace ILS as the global standard precision approach aid at the turn of the century. Pictured during trials at Hamilton Airport in Canada are an MLS elevation transmitter (foreground), which replaces the ILS glide slope antenna (left)....
MICRONAV INTERNATIONAL INC

Below: .... and an MLS azimuth transmitter which is dwarfed by the ILS localiser antenna.
MICRONAV INTERNATIONAL INC

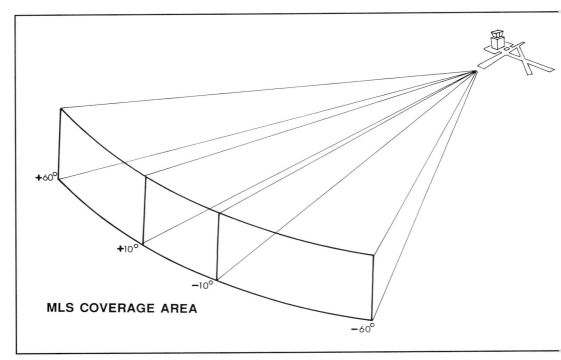

MLS COVERAGE AREA

+60°

+10°

−10°

−60°

busy airports already guide aircraft late on to the ILS localiser, in effect creating a curved approach, but using visual radar surveillance rather than the ILS to provide lateral and vertical guidance in the early part of the approach.

In theory, it would also be possible for a larger number of aircraft to use MLS simultaneously than can currently use ILS (because ILS is so narrow, aircraft must follow each other down the glide path, maintaining predetermined separations) and thereby increase capacity. But the reality is that all those aircraft must still land on the same runway, with its separation requirements and handling constraints, meaning that the landing system as a whole will only be able to handle as many aircraft as existing ILS systems. It will, however, enable controllers to use steep and curved approaches to more efficiently sequence aircraft into the system, and it will provide a precision approach capability for airports which are hindered by natural or man-made obstructions from installing ILS.

The International Civil Aviation Organisation (ICAO) has decreed that until 1 January 1998, both ILS and MLS will be the standard non-visual aids to approach and landing, by which time, all major international airports should be equipped with MLS. A two-year transition period will then follow when MLS becomes the primary system, with ILS being phased out. As from 1 January 2000, MLS will be the sole ICAO standard aid to approach and landing, with ILS being completely withdrawn from international service.

However, continued reluctance on the part of the aviation industry to adopt MLS is forcing ICAO to rethink its plans for MLS implementation.

Airports are reluctant to invest in the new equipment because, despite earlier hopes, it does not seem that MLS will in fact generate additional capacity. And it will only be effective once the airline have installed MLS receivers in their aircraft.

At present, the airlines are reluctant to make this substantial investment for a number of reasons. In the first place, replacing ILS equipment with MLS is expensive, and it entails installing yet another 'box' in the flightdeck. Airlines are being bombarded with requirements to install new 'boxes' — they must carry ILS, will be required to carry MLS, in the United States they must carry 'Traffic Collision Avoidance Systems' (TCAS), and they will be required to carry 'Automatic Dependent Surveillance' (ADS) equipment. And, with the advent of satellite navigation systems, they will increasingly be required to carry those as well, and there is likely to be a long and expensive transition period between the old and the new systems when flightdecks are crammed with multiple redundant systems to provide a comprehensive overlap.

In the second place, MLS will not be effective until a sufficient number of airports have installed the system to make it worthwhile for the airlines' to invest. A chicken-and-egg situation is fast developing. The international aviation community is largely hedging its bets on future satellite-based systems to replace most — if not all — ground-based navaids and there is a fear that systems like MLS and TCAS will be obsolete before it has been possible to recoup investment costs.

As a result, ICAO is to hold a major meeting in 1995 to review the question of MLS implementation.

In the meantime, during the transition period when MLS is being installed on runways which are already equipped with ILS, care has to be taken to avoid mutual interference between the two systems.

RVR

Not a radio-based system at all, but a key part of the precision approach equation, the 'Runway Visual Range' (RVR) is the final link for getting an aircraft on to the runway during conditions of poor visibility. There are two basic elements which make up the criteria for the various operational categorisation of runways. One is a vertical or height decision and dictates the height at which the pilot must either make visual contact with the runway or abandon the

approach and execute a 'go-around'. The other is a lateral or distance decision which dictates the minimum forward visibility requirements on the runway once the aircraft is on the ground. If the pilot is unable to see the runway ahead of him, the aircraft could veer off the asphalt, threatening not only the safety of all on board, but also potentially the safety of other aircraft and ground vehicles.

Runway visibility is measured by an instrument called a transmissometer. This consists of a light source which is projected on to a photocell a few yards away. By measuring the amount of light that is actually received by the photocell and comparing that to the amount projected over a standard distance, the instrument can calculate the visibility.

As visibility levels can vary along the length of the runway, RVR units are installed at both ends of the runway and in the middle and all three readings or a single average are transmitted to the pilot. Only when all three are within the ICAO specified minimum range can the aircraft land. RVRs are usually activated and information passed to pilots when visibility drops below 1,500ft.

RADIO AIDS TO COMMUNICATION

Until fairly recently, all communication between aircraft and air traffic control has relied on voice communications transmitted via radio waves. For the purposes of air traffic control, all radiotelephony or R/T is conducted using the VHF (Very High Frequency) or HF (High Frequency) bands. Both bands have properties that make them suitable for particular uses.

HF

HF has much longer range than VHF, but is very vulnerable to static interference which makes it a very noisy communications system. And, in addition to the static, it is extremely busy, largely as a result of its long-range capabilities. Over Central Asia, for example, HF transmissions can be heard from as far afield as Cairo and Singapore. So the airwaves are not only noisy, but cluttered and congested as well.

These problems are only compounded, particularly in developing regions, by the use of outdated and poorly maintained transmission and receiving equipment. As a result, communications are often distorted and garbled. Pilots, who travel the routes frequently and know what sort of instructions or messages to expect, can usually decipher what is being said but, to the inexperienced ear, HF wavebands sound like a cacophony of incomprehensible sounds. Parts of Africa and the Indian subcontinent are particularly notorious for their poor ATC communications.

If it is not possible for an aircraft to transmit a required position report because it is not within range of a suitable transmitter, the message may be passed to another aircraft which is within range and which will pass on the position report to the ground station.

Alternatively, the aircraft may be within range of a listening ground station which can then pass messages by telephone to the relevant air traffic control unit. Air traffic controllers in the Seychelles, for example, in the middle of the Indian Ocean, often relay messages into regions of Africa where radio reception is so poor that it is often impossible for aircraft to raise any contact with ATC units on the ground. From as far north as Cairo, pilots travelling north-south over the African continent may eventually resort to calling the Seychelles for transmission of messages ground-to-ground to *en route* centres they are unable to raise from the air.

The Seychelles, like many other regions which rely on HF transmissions, has introduced a 'Selcal' (Selective Calling) system which means that the flight crew need not monitor the noisy HF frequencies in case there is a call for them. If a Selcal-equipped ground station needs to communicate with a particular aircraft, it dials that aircraft's Selcal code and a bell chimes in the cockpit to alert the flight crew that they are wanted on the radio. Likewise, the airborne crew can use Selcal to contact the ground.

It allows for a much quieter working environment. Air traffic controllers, however, are still required to monitor the noisy airwaves to keep a mental eye on the whereabouts of aircraft in their region and keep track of aircraft entering and leaving the area or not equipped with compatible systems. Pilots, too, will often monitor the HF band to track all traffic within their vicinity. And if Selcal is not available, the crew must monitor the HF frequencies in any case to listen out for any calls. On occasions, however, static and other interference is so bad that crews cannot distinguish calls for them or are unable to understand instructions transmitted.

VHF

VHF has a shorter range (approximately 200nm) and is also subject to the line-of-sight rule, but it is almost totally unaffected by static interference and therefore provides a clear line of communication. VHF is most commonly used where range permits, and is used in such navaids as VOR and the ILS localiser beam. To ensure comprehensive coverage of VHF transmission, relay stations or additional transmitters must be sited along even the most remote parts of a route. This is often logistically impossible and invariably expensive, which is why many regions still rely on HF.

However, with increasing demand for VHF bands for commercial and domestic radio transmissions, there is now a shortage of frequencies in some areas — particularly in the US and some parts of Europe — and interference in the aviation bands from commercial and domestic broadcasts is increasing. Hence the growing demand for a system such as MLS to replace ILS.

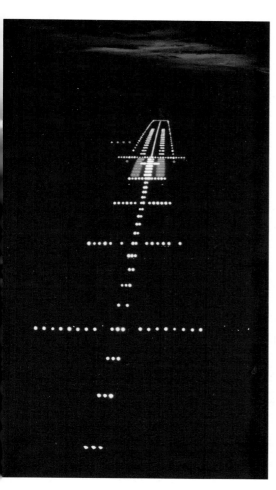

Above: **An airport's automated landing category is determined by the sophistication of its instrument landing aids and by the complexity and intensity of its runway lighting. This configuration at Luton Airport includes white approach lights and crossbars, banks of red lights in the undershoot zone, green lights to denote the threshold, and white runway edge, runway centreline, and touchdown zone lights. A row of red lights marks the far end of the runway which is also equipped with PAPIs to the left of the runway edge.**
SIMON-PARMEKO

Datalink

Voice communication has three basic disadvantages: it is time-consuming, subject to interference, and prey to the vagaries of regional accents. In dense traffic areas, it is essential that the pilot and controller are able to pass and receive messages quickly and precisely. If several pilots try to transmit messages at the same time, only one will be received by the controller, and the other pilots must wait their turn to send their messages. An urgent transmission may have to wait

until there is a gap in communications. As traffic levels increase, so too does the amount of air-ground communication and congestion of the airwaves can be a problem, particularly during peak periods.

To help relieve these problems, air-ground messages are increasingly sent in the form of data. A message from the ground will be transmitted to the aircraft's computer and reach the pilot through the aircraft's 'Flight Management System' (FMS). Cockpits will increasingly be equipped with small printers which can print out a hard copy of instructions for the pilot. Similarly, the pilot can send data messages back to the surface. The system is known as datalink and will increasingly replace voice communications as the primary air-ground communications link. It has the advantage of being an extremely fast method of transmission — data travels much faster than voice — and automatically includes such crucial information as the identity of the aircraft from which it is being sent. It is less susceptible to corruption and is completely immune to the vagaries of accent.

As Flight Management Systems become increasingly sophisticated and air traffic control procedures become more automated, aircraft will simply transmit regular and routine position reports automatically to ground computers without reference to the pilot, a process known as Automatic Dependent Surveillance. Voice communications will only be used when an immediate response to a request or instruction is required.

VISUAL AIDS TO NAVIGATION

These days, visual aids are restricted primarily to runway lights and visual approach aids such as PAPIs or VASIs.

Runway lighting

Airports are categorised according to their operational standard and it is this categorisation which dictates the type and size of aircraft that may operate there, and the minimum operational conditions which apply. Factors that might affect an aircraft's ability to operate into a particular airport include the runway length, the altitude of the airport, and the availability of emergency services in the event of an accident, plus such bad weather considerations as the accuracy and reliability of the ILS, and the visibility and configuration of the runway lighting system.

Some smaller airfields or strips have no runway lighting at all and are therefore operational only during daylight, while others may possess just centreline lights or runway edge lights or a basic combination of both. Commercial airports have much more sophisticated runway lighting arrangements. A comprehensive array at a major airport, for example, would include white runway edge and centreline

Above: **A KLM Boeing 747 descends over the runway approach lighting on target for the touch down zone.**
NOLTE

lights, banks of white approach lights (sometimes equipped with a 'follow-me' series of flashing strobes), white crossbars for axis reference, banks of red lights indicating the undershoot zone, green threshold indicators, white touchdown zone lights, and — where relevant — elevated snow lights.

VASIs and PAPIs

'Visual Approach Slope Indicators' (VASIs) consist of two (or three at airports where the traffic mix includes heavy, widebodied aircraft) symmetrically positioned banks of lights on both sides of the runway, bracketing the origin point of the glidepath on the runway centreline in the touchdown zone. The lights, usually three to a row, are angled so as to indicate to the pilot whether he is above, below or exactly on the glideslope. If the pilot is making his approach at the correct angle, he will see a row of red lights above a row of white lights. If he is too high, he will see all white lights, and if he is too low, all red lights. By

adjusting his rate of descent, he can recapture the correct glideslope.

If there are less than three lights to each row, or the VASIs are positioned only on one side of the runway, the system is known as an abbreviated VASI or AVASI.

Today, VASIs are being replaced with 'Precision Approach Path Indicators' (PAPIs) which consist of a single row of four lights positioned on one or both sides of the runway. On the correct glidepath, the pilot will see two red lights nearest the runway, flanked by two white lights. The lights can then identify two levels of error: three white lights and one red indicate that the aircraft is slightly high, while a bank of four whites warns that the aircraft is too high. Similarly three reds and a white indicate that the aircraft is just below the glidescope, while four reds warn that it is well below.

PAPIs offer numerous advantages over VASIs. VASIs tend to give an oscillatory approach, are imprecise below 200ft, and are of no help if a non-standard approach is used. In addition, colours can be difficult to distinguish during hazy weather conditions and the units need constant checking and maintenance to ensure accuracy.

PAPIs on the other hand consist of sealed units

emitting a bicoloured white-over-red beam. These units are easier to install and maintain, not subject to the same oscillation as VASIs, capable of multi-path interpretation, and are more precise and flexible than the older VASIs. Most airports are now replacing their VASIs with PAPIs.

Above: **Final approach into Tokyo's Narita Airport, showing the PAPIs to the left of the runway indicating that the aircraft is maintaining the correct glideslope.**

Below: **Runway 05 at Stansted, with the ILS localiser beacon for runway 23 in the foreground and the glideslope antenna for runway 05 to the left of the strip next to the PAPIs.**

9. FLIGHT PLANNING

Aircraft these days navigate along a predetermined route using an 'Inertial Navigation System' (INS). This is a self-contained airborne unit which requires no reference to external signals of any description. It senses aircraft movement through onboard accelerometers on an inertial platform stabilised by gyroscopes. Gyroscopes align themselves with True North, but always remain in a fixed position in space and level with the earth's surface. The accelerometer senses any acceleration or deceleration and passes the signal to a computer which can convert this data into velocities and distances relative to a specified starting point. It therefore knows at all times where the aircraft is and calculates what heading it should take to keep on the proposed track.

All aircraft journeys are broken down into a series of 'way points' which, although they have been given official names, are often nothing more than a set of map co-ordinates. On occasions, the name of a way point may relate directly to a landmark or region immediately below it. Some are radio beacons and some are official ATC reporting points, but most are just imaginary points delineating a map reference. They are used to guide the navigation system along the route, to monitor progress along that route and, particularly on long journeys, to enable the pilots to check the accuracy of the INS, which even on the longest journeys is usually very reliable — provided the correct co-ordinates are fed into the system prior to departure to give the INS an accurate starting reference point.

Each route, therefore, is made up of a series of way points. A journey from Hong Kong to London via the Middle East, for example, will route via up to 90 way points.

Until recently, and the advent of highly automated and sophisticated flight management and information systems, the flight crew were responsible for programming the co-ordinates of way points into the INS. As a general rule, the systems could handle up to nine 13-digit co-ordinates at any one time. The pilot, first officer and flight engineer (as relevant) would

Left: **Despite plans for greater automation of flight plan processing, controllers still favour working with manual flight strips to keep track of the aircraft under their control. Jersey Airport.**
PHILIPS

monitor their individual INS terminals as one member of the crew fed in each set of 13-digit co-ordinates and programmed the system. It was a time-consuming procedure and one which — despite the cross-referencing of three people in the flight deck — could generate navigation errors. One wrong number could lead the aircraft off track.

Nowadays, however, standard flight plans are programmed into the onboard computers and the pilot in command simply selects the routeing he has elected to fly and the way point co-ordinates are already stored in the computer's memory. As long as the aircraft is on autopilot, the aircraft will track its way from co-ordinate to co-ordinate unless the flight crew feeds in an override command to alter or update way points in the event of a detour *en route*. The pilot may, for example, request a detour to avoid a patch of bad weather or be routed away from a particularly busy sector of airspace to increase separation.

This increased INS automation has significantly reduced the flight crew workload, especially necessary in view of the fact that most of today's modern jets are operated with a two-man instead of the more traditional three-man flight crew.

Flight plans

Before each flight, an official flight plan has to be filed with the air traffic control authorities at the airport where the flight is originating. This is then processed into a format acceptable to air traffic controllers and distributed to all air traffic service providers along a flight's intended route. For airlines, the purpose of flight planning is to determine how long a flight will take and how much fuel will be needed. In their ATC application, flight plans alert each air traffic control centre of a flight's intended passage through its airspace so that appropriate arrangements can be made to ensure that that flight can be handled as requested.

A busy centre will handle hundreds of flight plans each day and will ensure that sufficient manpower and technical resources are on hand to be able to process safely all those flights. If, for any reason, a centre is short of the required resources, it will define its handling limitations and notify those to all affected ATC centres. If a particular flight plan conflicts with that centre's safety limitations, the centre may reject the flight plan, in which case it may have to be refiled with new timings or the aircraft diverted away from that particular centre. Alternatively, the aircraft can be

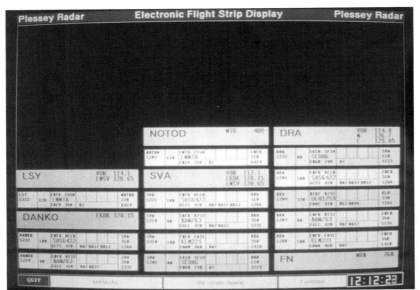

Left: In the future, flight strips will be increasingly automated, displayed on screen and with all information automatically distributed to air traffic control centre's along an aircraft's route by computer. These can be displayed on a dedicated screen or window, ...
SIEMENS PLESSEY SYSTEMS

Below: .... or brought into the main display if the controller needs to obtain immediate additional information about flights operating within his/her airspace.
SIEMENS PLESSEY SYSTEMS

Right: For the time being, however, controllers are keen to retain the manual flight strips.

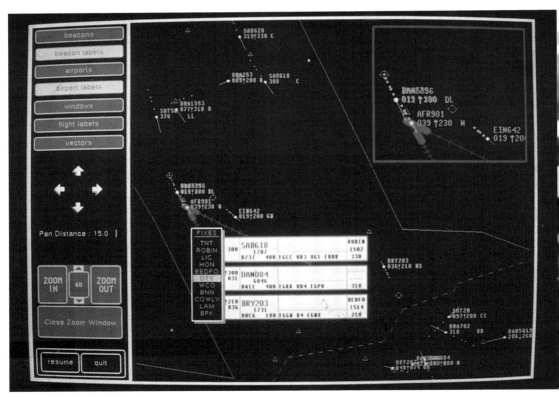

instructed to maintain a slower cruise speed to delay its arrival over a particular sector.

All flight plans used to be manually processed, with the relevant information written by hand on to flight strips, and transmitted between control centres in the form of teletype messages, using AFTN ('Aeronautical Fixed Telecommunications Network' — a dedicated aeronautical operations telex-type communications system). Today, the entire process is increasingly automated.

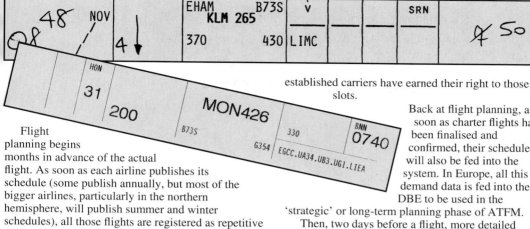

Flight planning begins months in advance of the actual flight. As soon as each airline publishes its schedule (some publish annually, but most of the bigger airlines, particularly in the northern hemisphere, will publish summer and winter schedules), all those flights are registered as repetitive flight plans. This assumes that, for a predetermined period, those flights listed will operate between the specified points on the specified days and at the specified times: those scheduled airlines are in effect making advance bookings on airspace slots.

At the busiest airports, airlines will also have to hold scheduling slots for each flight: that is, a predetermined departure or take-off 'window.' At London Heathrow, for example, an airline may be licensed to operate at Heathrow, have access to ground facilities and services arranged, and hold the traffic rights to operate a certain route. But without a slot, it cannot operate that service. The airport day is divided up into a number of slots which represent the number of aircraft the runways can handle. Every departing and arriving flight must, therefore, be allocated a slot to ensure that not all flights are trying to arrive at the same time of day, leaving other periods vastly underutilised.

Slot allocation at European airports remains somewhat random and, at the busiest airports, new airlines in particular are finding it very difficult to obtain anything but the least desirable slot times, which means that they cannot compete against the established carriers who already hold the most favourable slots. In addition, the airlines have always assumed ownership of the slots, selling them on as valuable assets if the holding airline or certain sectors of it are sold to another airline. The sale of Pan Am's London operation, including its prime Heathrow slots, to United Airlines highlighted the unwieldy dilemma behind the slot allocation process.

In the case of Europe's most heavily congested airports, slots are now such valuable assets that many airport operators argue that they should retain ownership and the right to allocate.

Work is under way to establish some sort of European standard for more transparent slot allocation and a resolution of the dilemma over whether new entrants should have access to prime slots or whether established carriers have earned their right to those slots.

Back at flight planning, as soon as charter flights have been finalised and confirmed, their schedules will also be fed into the system. In Europe, all this demand data is fed into the DBE to be used in the 'strategic' or long-term planning phase of ATFM.

Then, two days before a flight, more detailed checks are made on the status of that flight and any last minute changes notified by the aircraft operators. Barring any unforeseen technical problems or weather setbacks, that flight is now confirmed to operate as intended. In the European ATFM system, this is known as the 'pre-tactical' planning phase and interfaces the updated DBE demand data, last minute changes and other archived data with the latest information about capacity available in the ACCs.

From this combined data, the five FMUs which make up CEU West draw up a plan which defines the restrictions to be applied to traffic flows on the day concerned. This information is published in the middle of each day in the form of an 'ATFM Notification Message' (ANM) which is despatched to more than 1,000 addressees (both air traffic control centres and aircraft operators). The ANM describes in a single message all the tactical ATFM measures which will be in force on the following day.

On the actual day of the flight, a much more detailed plan is drawn up. From an airline point of view, selecting the exact final flight plan and preferred flight levels *en route* can be affected by a number of factors, the two most significant of which are the weather and congestion.

Weather

Weather conditions can have a major effect on last minute flight planning. If there is particularly bad weather at some point along a route, an aircraft may request a diversion to avoid it. This may take the aircraft off the standard routing, into an alternative Control Zone. If that Control Zone is capacity-restricted for the period of time that the aircraft anticipates arriving at its boundary, a time must be found when it is suitable for that aircraft to enter that airspace. The flight plan may, therefore, be rejected subject to revised timings.

If the weather is particularly hot at the take-off point and the aircraft heavily loaded, the aircraft will

Above: **Manual flight strips are likely to remain a feature of air traffic control operations for some time to come, if only as a back-up in the event of a computer failure.**
SIEMENS

take longer to climb to its preferred cruising altitude. This may mean that it is unable to climb above a constrained or restricted area of airspace and, as a result, it may have to accept a delay or a diversion.

Indeed, if the weather is very hot, the performance of the aircraft may be adversely affected to the point where payload (cargo or passengers) must be offloaded in order to enable the aircraft to get airborne and complete its journey. If the flight is to be an ultra long-haul non-stop journey, the aircraft will need every drop of fuel it can carry, but because it is so heavy when it takes off, it is actually burning fuel at a greater rate in the early part of the journey (using fuel to carry fuel) — especially in the initial climb phases — than it will when some of the fuel has been used up and the aircraft becomes lighter.

Payload may also have to be offloaded if temperatures affect the amount of fuel to be loaded. In high temperatures, fuel density is lower than in low temperatures so that the volume of fuel which can be loaded is less when the temperature is high. If the aircraft is unable to load a sufficient volume of fuel to get airborne and complete its non-stop journey, additional payload may have to be offloaded to decrease the overall weight of the aircraft.

Wind, at all stages of the flight, may have an affect on the overall flight plan. A strong favourable wind on departure may give a better rate of climb out after take-off, while *en route* winds can make the difference between a flight arriving late or early.

Depending on where they are and which direction they are travelling, most east-west flights will

encounter either a tail wind or a headwind. Aircraft take off and land into wind, to maximise lift, but once at cruise height will make better way with a tailwind. On a long flight, a strong headwind can add anything up to 1.5hr to a journey, while the same tailwind could significantly boost the speed of an aircraft going in the opposite direction.

Winds vary at different heights, so an aircraft may request an unusual flight level if it means avoiding a strong headwind.

Congestion, restrictions, and weather are therefore all taken into account when the Commander and his crew check in for a briefing at Flight Operations prior to a flight. The operations team will have assessed the conditions *en route* and the various options that may be available in terms of routeings, flight levels and destination alternates (alternative airfields within range of the aircraft at the end of its route, should its intended airfield be closed by bad weather or some other incident. The alternates must be equipped to handle the type and size of aircraft in terms of runway length, ground support and passenger handling equipment, and emergency services back-up.)

As the person taking ultimate and sole responsibility for the flight, the commander — usually the captain — takes the final decision on which plan to follow and that flight plan is then despatched to the local ATC centre and from there distributed — usually by AFTN — to all control centres along the route.

The captain receives a print-out of the flight plan which details the departure sequence and then each way point along the route. This is used by the operational crew to monitor the aircraft's progress along the route and to estimate arrival times at various reporting points. If the aircraft does not arrive at those points by the estimated times, it may mean that the aircraft is making slower progress than planned which could indicate stronger than calculated winds, or a technical problem. This could affect fuel burn and the aircraft's ability to arrive at its destination with its full legal load of additional fuel to allow for holds or diversions.

Most of these calculations are now done by onboard computers and there is less and less use of manual flight sheets. With many aircraft now reduced to two-man flight crew operations, this reduction in navigation workload leaves the crew additional time to monitor the progress and performance of the aircraft and maintain a constant stream of often vital ATC communications.

Most control centres are now equipped with computerised flight plan processing systems which automatically process the flight plan data into an ATC format. Repetitive flight plans from larger airlines are generally received on magnetic tapes or disks, but AFTN messages are still used in certain circumstances.

Until the aircraft receives an ATC clearance just prior to departure, the flight plan is still only a request for a particular routeing and flight level, although for scheduled services, approval is usually routine. An ATC clearance means that, in principle, the flight plan has been approved, but communication to some regions is so slow that an objection from one sector of the flight to the proposed flight plan may only be received after the aircraft has already departed. Re-routeings, flight level changes, speed restrictions or radar vectoring may be built into the flight plan *en route* to ensure separations are maintained as necessary.

In each control centre, the flight plan is received into the local flight plan processing system and checked for syntax. The sector of the flight affecting that flight plan processing system's ATC facilities is extracted and stored in the system's memory. It contains such information as flight number, aircraft callsign, registration and type, airport of departure, destination, nominated alternates, routeing, requested flight level, estimates, the aircraft's air speed, Selcal code, and radio equipment carried.

About 30min before the flight is due to arrive at the boundary of the first of the flight plan processing system's ATC facilities, the latest data on that flight (estimated entry time, latest altitude, and present SSR transponder code or 'squawk') is fed into the system via direct computer data link. In order to do this, the flight plan processing systems must be fully compatible. Where they are not, the updated information must be manually fed in using data transmitted by phone from the previous ATC unit.

Once the updated information has been fed into the flight plan processing system, it automatically prints a flight plan strip for that sector of the flight. It also automatically associates a radar target with its associated flight plan, using the SSR transponder code for identification, and presents this information to the controller on his radar display screen. In essence, however, despite all the detail that goes into flight planning, in reality, there are so many variables, particularly on a long flight, that can affect planned estimates, that aircraft are handled as they arrive and separation problems solved by the local controller.

The flight strip is a narrow piece of paper on which is printed details of the flight and on which the controller can mark any requests for changes to routeings or flight levels, plus any controller instructions such as reporting points and estimates over those points. For convenience sake the flight strip is mounted in a plastic holder, and as he 'accepts' or assumes responsibility for an aircraft about to enter his sector, the controller will activate the flight strip relating to that aircraft by adding it to his strip panel.

Controllers use the strips as a means of monitoring the progress of each aircraft through their airspace, and for sequencing aircraft into and through that airspace. If for any reason an aircraft does not make a position report at the time estimated, the controller is alerted to the possibility that something is wrong with that aircraft. If he is unable to restore contact with that aircraft, the controller will duly activate emergency procedures.

If all goes according to plan, however, the controller hands on the aircraft to the next control centre and the strip relating to that aircraft is removed from his panel.

With the increasing use of computers in ATC, there is a great deal of research development being done into the full automation of flight strips on to the radar screen. At present, a shortage of SSR transponder codes is hindering this process — there are currently only 4,096 codes available for the more than 200,000 flights operated each day — but the introduction of 'Mode Select' (or 'Mode S') transponders will solve this problem. Mode S has 16.7 million codes available which means that each aircraft will be able to have a dedicated code associated with its registration.

In theory, it will ultimately be possible to do away with flight strips and rely solely on automated screen strip displays. However, there is some controller resistance to doing away with strips. Not only do they provide a solid form of back-up in the event of a computer failure, but they are also often retained as legal documents in the event of an incident or accident investigation. It seems likely that they will remain a feature of air traffic control centres for some time to come.

10. THE FUTURE

The future for air traffic control lies in the stars. Satellite-based systems provide the key for ICAO's 'Future Air Navigation Systems' (FANS) concept for global CNS.

Satellite systems use special navigation satellites to establish the whereabouts of each aircraft. At present there are two primary constellations of satellites under development — GPS and GLONASS.

GPS

The GPS or 'Global Positioning System' is a network of 24 satellites developed and put into orbit by the US Department of Defense (DoD). It was originally developed for military purposes and provides a highly accurate system of navigation, which was proven during the Gulf conflict in 1991. The entire constellation was due to come on line with an 'Initial Operational Capability' (IOC) in the summer/early autumn of 1993. The last of the 24 satellites was launched in May 1993, and completion of an upgrade of the entire network to new generation satellites is scheduled for completion in 1995.

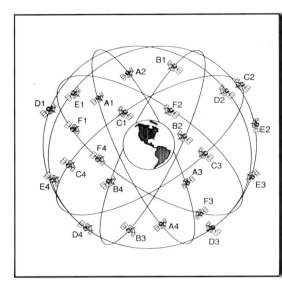

Above left: **The GPS satellite constellation of 21 operational plus three standby satellites.**
FAA

Left: **On the flightdeck of the Boeing 747-300.**

Above: **A British Airways Boeing 747 climbs away from Heathrow.**

Twenty-one of the satellites are operational, with three standbys, and together the network will provide coverage over most of the earth's surface. The US government has promised that the world's civil aviation sector can have access to the satellites free of charge for at least the first 10 years of operation, ie until 2003. In the meantime, the US will retain overall control of the network and provide maintenance and development. Because of the network's military role, the US DoD has insisted that GPS signals are to be deliberately degraded, limiting the accuracy available to civil users to about 100m. This is known as 'Selective Availability' or SA *(see also Chapter 11, Accuracy).*

The satellites themselves have an estimated life span of seven years each, but the earliest satellite has now been in orbit for almost 10 years and is still fully operational. Only one satellite has been lost since the launch programme began. The accuracy offered by the satellites is achieved through the incorporation of highly precise and reliable atomic clocks and it is a failure in this unit, more than any other, that is adversely affecting a similar satellite network currently under development in Russia.

GLONASS

The 'Global Orbiting Navigation Satellite System' is a complementary 24-satellite constellation developed initially by the communist regime of the former Soviet Union in response to the US system. Its future remains somewhat uncertain due to the continuing political instability in the region. It is uncertain, for example, whether there are sufficient resources to complete the development programme and sustain essential satellite replacements in the future.

It is understood that a major launch programme was planned for 1993 and Russia remains committed to having the GLONASS constellation completed and fully operational as scheduled by 1995.

At present, the life expectancy of the GLONASS satellites is little more than two years. In total, Russia and the Soviet Union before it have launched more than 60 satellites since launches began in 1982. But there have never been more than 15 or 16 satellites operational at any one time.

Russia has promised that its system will be available to the civil aviation sector free of charge for the first 10 to 15 years of operation. Unlike its US

counterpart, the Russian military forces have not insisted that GLONASS signal accuracy be downgraded for civil use: Selective Availability will not be a feature of the GLONASS constellation.

There is no doubt that the redundancy offered by having 48 satellites instead of just the 24 GPS units would significantly improve the reliability and availability of the system and the GLONASS network is therefore a very desirable addition. Already, research and development work is under way to develop satellite transceivers for aircraft that would be able to work with both GPS and GLONASS satellites. However, integrating the two systems is likely to be an expensive project because they use different time references. Each GLONASS satellite has been allocated its own frequency for purposes of identification, whereas the GPS satellites all use the same frequency, but have been allocated separate identification codes.

Ownership

The biggest hurdle to the implementation of either GPS or GLONASS is the political implication of the world's civil aviation community becoming wholly reliant upon systems that are owned and operated by the world's two military superpowers. Ownership issues as far as 'Global Navigation Satellite Systems' (GNSS) are concerned are still a long way from being resolved.

There is widespread anxiety that, in a military

crisis, the US or Russia could relocate satellites as required, to give greater coverage over a conflict zone, with the potential of reducing the cover available to civil aviation in certain regions; severely corrupt the degree of accuracy available to the civil sector; or indeed switch the system off altogether, leaving civil aviation in total chaos.

The Gulf conflict in 1991 served to highlight the problem. In order to maximise satellite coverage over the conflict zone, satellites from the southern hemisphere were reportedly relocated, leaving New Zealand and Australia with reduced cover.

In addition, there is concern over charging methods to be introduced after the 10-15 year grace period. Owning nations would then be in a position to impose any level of charges they felt appropriate for use of the satellite constellations. If the intention was to recover the initial cost of development of the system, for example, charges could be very high indeed. At that point, it seems likely the international civil aviation community would have little option but to absorb such costs. However, it is believed that the US government is already considering transferring operational authority of the GPS system from the Department of Defense (DoD) to a civil transport authority, such as the Federal Aviation Administration (FAA), a move that would in effect free the US and international civil aviation sectors from having to foot the bill for evelopment of the system. However, in view of the act that the system would still ultimately be owned by he US government, the DoD would inevitably have priority access in a military crisis.

A number of potential resolutions to the ownership and charges issues related to GNSS are currently being liscussed. One involves the transfer of ownership and control of both systems to an independent organisation, such as ICAO, for example. However, it eems likely in that case that the two powers which leveloped these systems would be looking for some sort of recompense for relinquishing key military hardware. This could cover the purchase cost of existing satellites or involve recovery of a significant proportion of the development costs — options which vould in essence put GNSS beyond the financial reach of civil aviation. But in reality much of the levelopment and satellite payload costs relate to acilities which have been designed solely for military use and have no civil application. The civil sector would inevitably be unwilling to pay for those. Experts believe that a dedicated civil system without any military trappings could cost less than 20% of GPS.

Left: **An aircraft descends over the ILS to land.**
MIAMI INTERNATIONAL AIRPORT

Below: **Tails at Heathrow.**
BAA PLC

If the US government does decide to absorb the development costs of the system and release the operational system to the FAA, transfer to an international body would be that much easier. A phased transition whereby the international body, through its members, would finance future satellite replacements and system maintenance is one possible option. Once all the existing US satellites have been replaced by those financed by the international body, the system would in effect be owned by the international civil aviation community.

In Europe, serious consideration is being given to the development of a dedicated civil GNSS. Eurocontrol has proposed European input into the GLONASS system to help fund satellite development, launch and replacement. However, GLONASS like GPS is burdened with military technology that has no civil application and would remain in essence a military tool. But, unlike GPS, the CIS military forces have no intention of deliberately downgrading system accuracy for civil use.

The Royal Institute for Navigation believes that what is needed is a satellite navigation system developed, owned, operated and controlled specifically for the benefit of the world-wide civil aviation community. Walter Blanchard, Chairman of the Institute's GNSS study group, cites INMARSAT, INTELSAT, and EUTELSAT as successful examples of supra-national organisations providing services for

Above: **A British Airways Airbus A320 gets airborne.**
AIRBUS INDUSTRIE

many different countries. They are all primarily communications systems alone, but INMARSAT is installing navigation facilities in its new generation satellites to complement the GPS/GLONASS constellations. In addition, proposals for Automatic Dependent Surveillance (ADS) trials using INMARSAT satellites are currently being studied.

Blanchard believes: 'GPS, etc, should be looked on more as technology demonstrators rather than anything else. They were developed for specific military applications and in the process were burdened with facilities and features quite inappropriate for a civil environment, not least being sheer cost. Their value lies in the active demonstration they provide of the successful development of satellite technology for navigation applications and the advantages it brings.'

He believes that the European Community should be 'easily capable of designing, building, launching, and operating its own satellite navigation system without any reference to GPS.'

The main problem with the INMARSAT option is that there would be fewer satellites available than in the GPS/GLONASS constellations. However, the Swedish Civil Aviation Authority, the Luftfartsverket, is working on a development that could reduce the number of satellites an aircraft would have to be able to 'see' in order to obtain accurate position data.

The system involves a GPS (ultimately to be a general GNSS) transponder, developed by Swedish inventor Håkan Lans, and a datalink communications enhancement synchronised with the atomic clocks in the satellites. By dividing each minute into 2,250 communications time slots, Lans believes it should be possible to handle all the air traffic in the world on a single 25kHz radio frequency. It is unlikely that there would be more than 2,250 aircraft operating within the same range area at any given time. Each time slot

would be used to transmit a datalink message which can contain a full position report, including identification, longitude, latitude, altitude, speed, direction and other status details.

As soon as a GPS transponder is switched on, it will try to locate a satellite and determine its position. The communication processor within the transponder will listen to the datalink frequency to determine what other traffic is in the vicinity and which time slots are free. Once it has determined the position of its own aircraft and made a dynamic 'telephone directory' of all other traffic, it makes its first transmission utilising one of the non-occupied time slots. The synchronised time slots are also used for transmitting differential corrections from the reference station.

Lans says: 'If no satellites at all are available — if for some reason, which is highly unlikely, the GPS system is turned off — it is possible to use position reports from the ground stations to determine the aircraft's position. With time synchronisation, it is possible to navigate on just one satellite. There will be other satellites, apart from GPS, available for time synchronisation purposes. However, if no satellites at all are available, a national atomic clock, which synchronises the ground stations in each country could be used to provide a completely independent back-up system for navigation.'

If the GPS receiver fails, it is still possible to navigate using the position report messages transmitted by other aircraft. Because the exact position of those aircraft is known, it is simply a matter of measuring the time it takes for their messages to arrive at the communications processor in order to determine the aircraft's exact position.

Accuracy is less precise than with the full satellite system, but time synchronisation does provide an independent back-up for as long as the ownership issues remain unresolved. And even when they are, time synchronisation will provide significant capacity enhancements to the datalink communications network.

11. GLOBAL NAVIGATION SATELLITE SYSTEMS

Satellite navigation is an airborne tool which involves aircraft and up to four satellites. A transceiver on the aircraft interrogates a satellite and calculates its position by measuring the length of time it takes for the reply to reach the aircraft.

The 24 satellites in the GPS constellation have been put into orbit so that each covers a large region of the earth's surface and overlaps with its neighbouring satellites to provide redundant coverage. At any point in its journey, an aircraft should be able to 'see' at least three and preferably four satellites. By obtaining a position report from each of these, the aircraft's navigation system receives a highly accurate three-dimensional position report giving its precise position, flight level, speed and heading. This report is more accurate than any that could currently be obtained using land-based technology.

At this point, the aircraft has made no communication with the ground; it has transmitted its own satellite interrogations and received the information independently of any land-based equipment. In order for air traffic control to receive the position data and provide surveillance and control services, the data must be transmitted to earth and this is done either by VHF radio or satellite voice or data links. At present, VHF remains the common communications tool, with satellite links still in the trial stage. But it seems likely that in future an increasing amount of air-to-ground communication will be datalink via satellite.

An automated system of position reporting will be

Below: **To obtain the most accurate position fix, an aircraft using Global Navigation Satellite Systems (GNSS) should ideally be able to interrogate four satellites. The accuracy of the position fix reduces in direct proportion to the number of satellites which the aircraft can 'see' at any one time.**
GP&C SYSTEMS

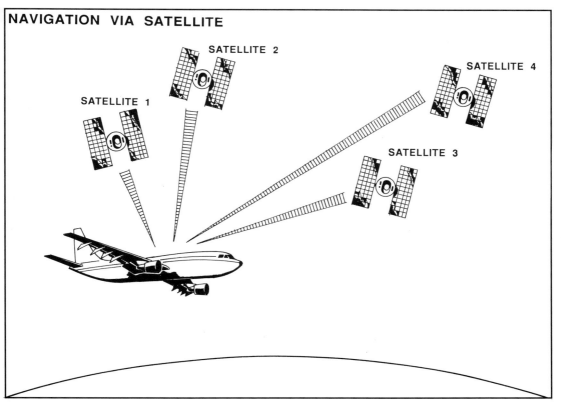

NAVIGATION VIA SATELLITE

SATELLITE 1

SATELLITE 2

SATELLITE 3

SATELLITE 4

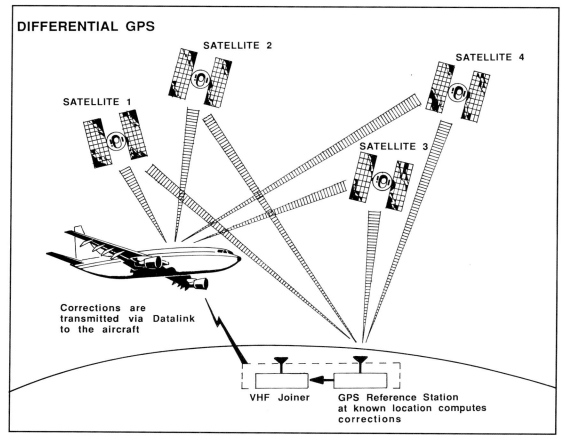

DIFFERENTIAL GPS

SATELLITE 1
SATELLITE 2
SATELLITE 3
SATELLITE 4

Corrections are transmitted via Datalink to the aircraft

VHF Joiner   GPS Reference Station at known location computes corrections

increasingly used worldwide, known as 'Automatic Dependent Surveillance' (ADS). With this system, the aircraft's computer automatically transmits position reports in the form of data in allocated time slots to land-based air traffic control computers. These reports constantly update the aircraft's position on the controller's synthetic picture.

Because the information he is receiving is much more accurate, the controller no longer has to allow margins of error for the data, and can therefore begin to reduce the separations between aircraft on his screen, particularly over oceans and deserts where visual surveillance has not previously been possible. For congested routes, like the popular North Atlantic airways, satellite-based systems will generate a significant increase in airspace capacity.

As another safety factor, the pilot can also receive a synthetic picture of the airspace in which he is flying which will detail the whereabouts of other aircraft in his vicinity and alert him of any potential collisions. There is some concern that this will encourage pilots to make their own decisions about safety margins and take corrective action independent of the air traffic controller — possibly jeopardising the controller's

overall plan. The intention is very clearly that ground-based air traffic controllers will retain control, but it is hoped that an extra airborne pair of eyes will help to further improve safety.

As with secondary surveillance radar, the one drawback of satellite systems is that they can only detect targets equipped with the appropriate interrogation/response equipment. A controller would be unaware of any aircraft flying within his airspace that were not GNSS transponder-equipped. It seems likely therefore that primary radar will continue to have a role to play.

Precision Approach Systems

Experts believe that satellite-based systems will ultimately be able to replace almost all the ground-based navigation and surveillance tools currently in use, including precision approach systems — and this is where the debate hots up and focuses on the potential drawbacks of a system which relies on highly sophisticated pieces of equipment orbiting the earth, miles above its surface.

Precision Approach Systems are necessary when the weather is bad enough to reduce visibility to the

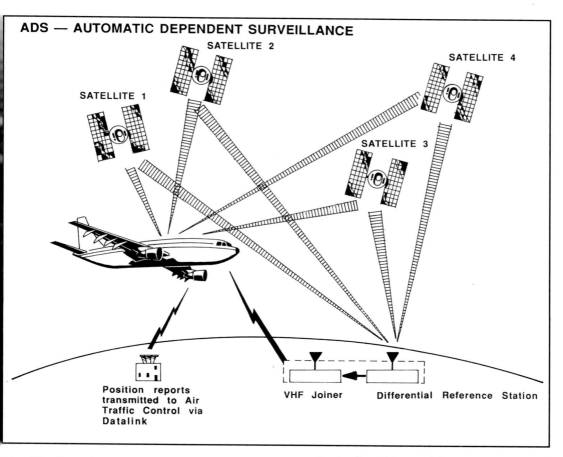

ADS — AUTOMATIC DEPENDENT SURVEILLANCE

SATELLITE 2

SATELLITE 4

SATELLITE 1

SATELLITE 3

Position reports transmitted to Air Traffic Control via Datalink

VHF Joiner

Differential Reference Station

Above left: **Differential GPS can be employed to overcome 'selective availability', a deliberate degradation of the accuracy available to civil users by the military operators of the US Global Positioning System (GPS). A computer on the ground, which knows its exact position, receives position fixes from aircraft and compares them with readings it is getting from the satellites. Because it knows its own position, it can calculate the amount of error being incorporated by the satellites, calculate the correction and transmit the corrected accurate position data back to the aircraft.**
GP&C SYSTEMS

Above: **For navigation purposes, aircraft talk to satellites without requiring any ground-based communications link. The entire navigational process is entirely airborne and therefore 'independent'. In order to let the air traffic controllers know where they are, aircraft transmit regular and automatic position reports via datalink to provide the ground surveillance link — known as automatic dependent surveillance or ADS.**
GP&C SYSTEMS

point where the pilot may not actually be able to see the runway until late in his approach — or possibly even not at all.

ILS (see Tools of ATC) has long been the industry-wide standard precision approach tool. But frequency congestion has forced the search for a replacement and MLS has been selected by ICAO as the most practical alternative. However, only a handful of air traffic control authorities — mainly in the US and Europe — are actively pursuing MLS implementation. For many authorities elsewhere, MLS is seen as a luxury they can ill afford. For many of them, airspace and frequency congestion is not a problem; they may have little need for Cat II/III precision approach aids and the cost of replacing perfectly serviceable equipment is high. As the debate over future precision approach aids continues, many air traffic service providers are pinning their hopes on global navigation satellite systems being able to provide a one-stop replacement for most ground-based navigational aids, including ILS.

GNSS

In theory, there is no reason why GNSS should not be used as a precision approach tool. Indeed, Swedish inventor Håkan Lans — better known perhaps for inventing colour computer graphics and the computer mouse — has been conducting trial precision approaches, using signals from GPS satellites and a transponder he developed himself, since 1988. But

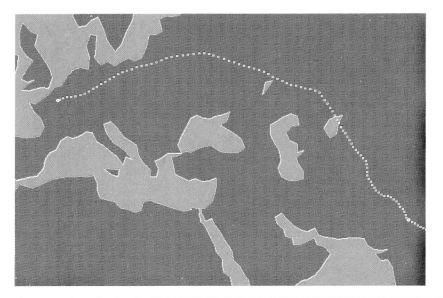

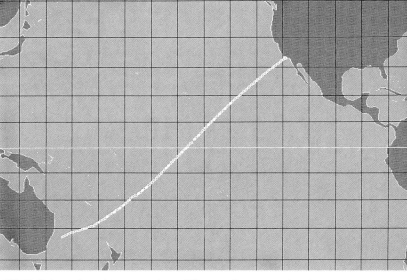

Left: **ADS trials providing precision aircraft tracking by satellite have so far proved very successful. This picture show the ADS tracking of a Cathay Pacific Airways flight from Asia to Paris in December 1992.**
ARINC/SITA

Below: **This shows the ADS tracking of a United Airlines flight from Los Angeles to Sydney in October 1992.**
ARINC/SITA

there are other schools of thought that doubt GNSS' precision approach capabilities on the grounds of accuracy, integrity, availability and reliability.

Accuracy

The problem of accuracy was relatively easy to solve, as Lans discovered. As has been already mentioned, the US GPS system was developed by the Department of Defense as a piece of military hardware. With its high degree of accuracy, it gave the US a military edge over its foes, and, in order to protect that edge, the US DoD is anxious that such precise levels of accuracy should not be available to other users. Because it is impossible to restrict access to the satellite system, the US opted to randomly apply what is known as 'selective availability' which reduces the level of accuracy available from the satellites. This will of course affect civil aviation. However, Lans and his team calculated that by using something called 'differential' GPS, they could eliminate SA inaccuracies from the system.

Differential GPS involves a series of ground-based reference stations which know precisely their own location. All ADS signals or other position reports from the aircraft are fed through those reference stations. When a reference station detects a deterioration in accuracy, it calculates the degree of the error and transmits a corrected position back to the aircraft. The position that the aircraft then transmits to the control centre is once again accurate, regardless of selective availability. The Swedish authorities believe that three or four such ground stations would be needed to provide differential cover for the whole of Sweden's airspace. Lans has been achieving accuracy of just a few metres, but believes that with refinement and the GPS system fully operational, accuracy of just a few centimetres is achievable.

At best, it will be some years before a final decision is reached.

Availability

Because the best possible picture is achieved if an aircraft can interrogate four satellites, it stands to reason that a smaller number of satellites reduces the levels of accuracy. In some parts of the world, it will only be possible to 'see' three satellites at one time. If one should fail, the degree of accuracy available for both navigation and precision approach work would be significantly reduced. In regions where four satellites are visible all the time, experts believe it will probably be possible to continue precision approach operations with just three satellites, although the aviation industry, being as safety conscious as it is, believes a three satellite configuration would allow no margin of redundancy.

If a satellite failed, an airport that could be offering full precision approach capability one minute might suddenly find it had lost a degree of accuracy the next which might mean it would have to shut down. In addition, not only would that satellite failure affect just that one airport, but also all the others in its vicinity that relied on that satellite. An aircraft arriving in bad weather might therefore find that not only was the precision approach capability at its destination airport out of order, but the same might also be true of its designated alternates.

However, the GPS satellites are not the only ones being launched. The Soviet-initiated GLONASS system will see a further 24 satellites operating to complement the GPS network. In addition, some communications satellites, including the most recent ones being launched by INMARSAT, will be equipped with a navigation capability.

Reliability

If a satellite does fail, it is virtually impossible to repair. And that is largely why satellites are such immensely expensive pieces of technology. Because it is not possible for technicians to reach and repair them, every onboard system is designed not to fail.

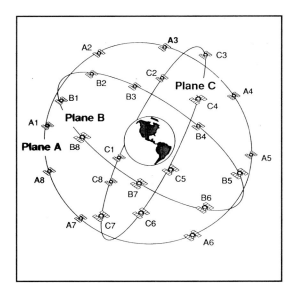

Above: **The proposed Russian GLONASS constellation of 21 satellites, due to be completed in 1995.**
FAA

The chance of failure therefore is remote, but if one does fail, how can it be replaced?

As has been described above, the GPS network consists of 21 operational satellites and three spares. In the event that a satellite fails somewhere in the network, the onboard rockets of one of the spares could be activated to send it into orbit to replace the failed unit.

But in reality, this would use up so much of the precious onboard energy reserves and thereby shorten the lifespan of the satellite that it is seen as a 'last resort' option. It is believed that there will eventually be sufficient satellites to ensure that full cover can be maintained in the event of a unit failure. The growing redundancy in the system created by the addition of extra satellite networks means that both availability and reliability are less of a problem.

Integrity

With existing ILS procedures, it is easy to establish — especially with the latest systems which electronically monitor their own sub-systems — whether a unit is working properly and providing the calibrated and required degree of accuracy. And if there is a problem, an engineer can attend to the problem instantly and repair the system within a short space of time.

It is less clear how quickly a satellite would either report or could be determined to have an onboard error and be transmitting false information.

However, the alternative satellite systems being launched will also help provide a monitoring service. The European Space Agency, for example, is planning to launch a network of geostationary satellites as an 'overlay' to the main system which, it is maintained, will be able to detect and alert any errors in the main system satellites in less than 10min.

Cost Benefits

Technically at least, it seems that perceived problems with accuracy, availability, reliability and integrity can in the long term be solved. More satellites giving greater redundant cover, the use of differential reference stations or the discontinuation of SA, plus the implementation of an overlay of monitoring satellites could ultimately ensure that GNSS replaces all existing ground-based navigation aids. But before that can happen, there are a great many political hurdles which will be more difficult to overcome.

By their very nature, satellites operate beyond the constraints of national boundaries and the ideal envisaged within the ICAO FANS concept is a truly global air traffic control system unhindered by regional sovereignty issues.

A major advantage of GNSS is that it requires little hardware investment on the ground. Airlines will need to shoulder the bulk of the investment burden, installing satellite transceivers in all their aircraft. National ATC authorities will need to invest in ground communications (data and voice) links, most commonly telephone lines, to their regional earth station, and possibly in differential ground stations (in the event that SA is retained) and/or potentially a national atomic clock.

Without the heavy costs associated with purchasing and installing a radar network and the related infastructure, nations — such as Third World and developing countries and the recently liberated Eastern European republics — which are currently struggling to provide efficient, effective and safe air traffic services in the face of growing traffic demand can quickly and cost effectively be brought up to the same standards as developed nations. It will be possible then to introduce global standards so that airlines will receive a seamless service no matter whether they are over the remotest ocean or transiting airspace of a cash-strapped developing nation.

In reality, however, as long as national boundaries exist on the ground, it seems inevitable that they will continue to exist in the air. But the air transport industry already enjoys an unprecedented level of international cooperation and it seems likely that it will pioneer a new era in global relations. For the time being at least, however, there are still a number of critical issues yet to be addressed, not least of which relates to civil/military ownership question. Only time will tell whether politicians have the vision to facilitate such a far sighted ideal.